Penguin Books

More on Oxymoron

Patrick Hughes is an artist who was born in England in 1939. He has lived in London and New York City. Mr. Hughes has written two previous books, *Upon the Pun: Dual Meaning in Words and Pictures* (with Paul Hammond) and *Vicious Circles and Infinity: An Anthology of Paradoxes* (with George Brecht), which is also published by Penguin Books.

The Unfindable
(Marcel Mariën)

MORE ON OXYMORON

Patrick Hughes

Penguin Books

Penguin Books Ltd, Harmondsworth,
Middlesex, England
Penguin Books, 40 West 23rd Street,
New York, New York 10010, U.S.A.
Penguin Books Australia Ltd, Ringwood,
Victoria, Australia
Penguin Books Canada Limited, 2801 John Street,
Markham, Ontario, Canada L3R 1B4
Penguin Books (N.Z.) Ltd, 182–190 Wairau Road,
Auckland 10, New Zealand

First published 1983

LIBRARY OF CONGRESS CATALOGING IN PUBLICATION DATA
Hughes, Patrick, 1939–
More on oxymoron.
Bibliography: p.
1. Figures of speech. 2. Visual perception. I. Title.
PN227.H83   1983   808   83-13050
ISBN 0 14 00.6786 8

Printed in the United States of America by
Fairfield Graphics, Fairfield, Pennsylvania
Set in Aster and Bauhaus
Designed by Beth Tondreau

Pages 207–208 constitute an extension of this copyright page.

To James Hughes

Contents

List of Illustrations

Acknowledgments

The author is very grateful to his editor, Patricia Mulcahy, for her faith in and help with this book, and to Lawrence Lawry for his photographs and support. He is grateful to the artists whose work is represented in this book for giving the author their permission to reproduce their work: Marcel Mariën, Anthony Earnshaw, Ian Hamilton Finlay (and his photographer, David Paterson), Tony Blundell, Bergentz, Saul Steinberg, Murray McDonald, Bianca Juarez, Ian Walker, Les Coleman, Glen Baxter, Maurice Henry, Jean Gourmelin, and Méret Oppenheim. If he has missed anyone, it is not intentional.

He is grateful to Scott Meredith Literary Agency and

Arthur Marx for permission to reprint from the latter's collection of Goldwynisms and to *The New York Times* and William Safire for permission to reprint from Mr. Safire's collection of self-exemplifications.

He would like to thank Hilary Rubinstein, George Brecht, Solomon Hughes, James Hughes, John Hughes, Molly Parkin, Paul Hammond, Liz Cowling, Matt Flowers, Walter Redfern, John Lyle, Dudley Winterbottom, Hamish McAlpine, Zoe Cardinal, Brad Faine, Angela Flowers, Trevor Winkfield, George Melly, Ivor Bowen, John Baldwin, Martin and Diane Ackerman, Shirley Cargill, David Sylvester, Steve Dove, Carol Wallitt, Phil Shaw, Nick Wadley, and Clive Philpot.

He is also grateful to Stanley Bard and the Chelsea Hotel.

Introduction

OXYMORON is itself an oxymoron. In Ancient Greek *oxus* means "sharp" and *moros* means "dull." Thus an oxymoron is a "sharp dullness." The terms are to be taken metaphorically: "sharp" as a metaphor for clever or wise, and "dull" as a metaphor for stupid or foolish. So oxymoron means "foolish wise" or "silly clever." It is the rhetorical figure in which two antithetical words are pitted against each other, adjective against noun, as in John Milton's **living death, loud silence,** or **darkness visible.**

When you consider the oxymoron you are also drawn to its opposite the PLEONASM, where the adjective agrees with the noun, as in **wet water** and **widow woman.** Then you consider these two terms amplified: the oxymoron extended turns into the CONTRA-

DICTION IN TERMS, and the extended pleonasm becomes the TAUTOLOGY.

The generic name for these kinds of use of language and logic is the BULL, a word whose etymology is cloudy. One of the definitions of bull offered by the *Oxford English Dictionary* is "a self-contradictory proposition." Both SELF-CONTRADICTION and SELF-REFERENCE are here. I have found four more distinct themes in bulls, which I have called OBVIOUS, FIGURE/GROUND REVERSAL, MIND AND MATTER, and NOTHING.

The *O.E.D.* has another definition: "A ludicrous inconsistency unperceived by the speaker." The bull has been called the Irish Bull in Britain, as if the colonized and (originally) Gaelic-speaking Irish had a monopoly on this wise foolishness. They are often called Polish jokes in the United States, after those immigrants; all over the world they have been named after different groups at different times. This is partly because those who are the butt of the joke are coming fresh to the language and using it broadly, without attending to any contradictions or ambiguities in the use of idiom. It is also because the immigrants are seen as having a novel approach to a problem, a reversal of the usual way of doing things: they are not hidebound. GOLDWYNISMS, phrases from Samuel Goldwyn, who came from Poland to England when he was twelve and to America when he was fifteen, are examined in the Appendix.

Besides written witticisms and anonymous jokes, *More on Oxymoron* also contains visual examples. As Alice says, "What is the use of a book without pictures?" One of the novelties of this book is the way it analyzes pictures in terms of verbal rhetoric. Pictorial language has been been much slower to be classified than its verbal equivalent, perhaps because it has only recently been freed by photography from the restraint of merely reproducing the world.

The variety of example here is important. We owe the word *cosmopolitan* to the Greek philosopher Diogenes. It is an oxymoron, taken from *cosmos* ("the world") and *politas* ("citizen") at a time when a citizen was expected to be a citizen of a city-state, not the whole world. I believe that the geographical, historical, and democratic variety shown in the material considered shows that this way of understanding is widespread.

As a child I was always dismayed by adult adulation of "common sense." It seems to me self-evident that the way of thinking displayed in these bulls is valid. When we smile at a joke or grin at a witticism, we are seeing a truth. I am obviously drawn to these kinds of remarks, and find them more accurate and realistic appraisals of the nature of reality than orthodox logic and language, where adjectives describe nouns, where the figure stands out clearly from the ground, where nothing is left to chance.

This is an amateur work, addressed throughout to the general reader and animated by love of the imagination. (I find Chomskyite linguistics and Barthesian structuralism disappointing.) Molière's *bourgeois gentilhomme* was delighted to learn that "for more than forty years I have been speaking prose without knowing it." I hope the various writers, comedians, artists, and cartoonists who have made these bulls would appreciate that they have been doing whatever it is I say they have been doing without knowing it. A common view of humor is that it is too light and elusive to write about. The argument is, here are amusements; do not weigh them down with weighty explanations. I take the view that here are profundities—how difficult to unravel them and still retain their meaning. It is like a book of poems "explained" in prose.

The philosopher Ludwig Wittgenstein said, "A serious work in philosophy could be written that consisted entirely of jokes."

MORE ON OXYMORON

1. Verbal
PLEONASM

I myself personally take pleonasm to be that form in which the
adjective or adverb has the same, or virtually the same, meaning
as its noun or verb:

poor paupers

wet water

unsuccessful failures

widow woman

enormous giant

new innovation

to visually see

to verbally tell

to physically pull

The etymology of pleonasm shows that it comes from the words *pleon*, meaning "more," and *pleos,* meaning "full." It means to be more superfluous, so it is itself a pleonasm. It might also be translated as a "moreism", as "moreish."

"Wet" is different from "water." A pleonasm is not necessarily a grammatical error; it is also a rhetorical emphasis. The qualities of a pleonasm are: to playfully and ironically underline a description (if made consciously); or to reveal the speaker's ignorance of the meaning of words (if made unconsciously).

2. Visual
PLEONASM

In the visual world, the noun part is taken by the thing and the adjective by the material of which the thing is constructed. A visual pleonasm is the toy seal (1). The noun is the seal, the adjective the sealskin, the remark translated into verbal language, **sealskin seal.** A real seal is made of sealskin; this miniature representation—some representations of things are smaller, some larger, some the

> What color is a red bus?

1. Sealskin Seal
(photograph by Lawrence Lawry)

same size—makes us especially aware that a seal is made of seal-skin by the difference in scale between toy seal and real skin. In a verbal pleonasm like **widow woman,** there may be a similar differ-ence in scale, there being more women than widows. The object is rather silly—real seals have been killed to make more toy ones. Reality has been raided to make its representation.

Consider also when water stands for water in adventure films of shipwrecks. The "toy" water in the sequences where a model ship is used in a tank seems a pleonasm, the waves created unnatural in their toylike motions. They are overresponsive, not weighty enough.

3. Verbal
TAUTOLOGY

Tautology comes from *tauto*, "the same," and *logos*, "saying." A tautology is something that is said again the same. When the two terms of the pleonasm are joined by a *copula*, it is a tautology. A copula is a linking verb that connects the subject and predicate of a sentence without asserting action; such verbs include "be," "look," "seem," "become," "appear." (*Copula* is Latin for "link.")

A lead article in Britain's *The Guardian* newspaper read:

At the center is the middle

Round the middle are the sides

The terms linked are "middle" and "center," and "round the middle" and "sides." "Middle" and "center" are synonyms; "round the middle" is a definition of "side." This is a piece of irony about

> What is a silver dollar made of?

the tautologous nature of middle-of-the-road political speech.

Politicians, wordy and cautious, are sometimes caught impromptu in tautologies that are humorous to the knowing observer:

"When large numbers of men are unable to find work, unemployment results." (Calvin Coolidge)

The humor can be deliberately achieved. Sheridan wrote:

The Spanish fleet thou canst not see—because—It is not yet in sight!

The unconscious solemnity of a local politician caught in tautological self-congratulation:

"One effect of the better lighting is the improved visibility."

Under the rubric *Colemanballs*, the satirical magazine *Private Eye* collects examples, with cruel intent, of the verbal "mistakes" made by athletes and sports commentators (largely untrained in rhetoric), as they struggle, on the air, to ride the radio or TV waves with relevant information:

"Thank you for evoking memories—particularly of days gone by." (Mike Ingham, BBC2-TV)

"Boycott, somewhat a creature of habit, likes exactly the sort of food he himself prefers." (Don Mosey, BBC Radio 3)

"Lillian's great strength is her strength." (David Coleman, BBC1-TV)

Tautology is not always silly. It can draw attention to the widest range of possibility:

The weather for catching fish is that weather, and no other, in which fish are caught. (W. H. Blake)

This remark is a contrast to some such remark as "You only catch bream when there has just been a heavy shower," which might put you off other possibilities.

Abraham Lincoln's **"For those who like this sort of thing, this is the sort of thing they like"** displays a profoundly fatalistic attitude. (The sentence is also a *chiasmus*, the rhetorical form in which the order of the phrases in the first part of the sentence is reversed in the second.)

Everything we like is the sort of thing we like. How do we come to like the things we do not like? There is a song by Henry Blossom with these lyrics: **I want what I want when I want it.**

The terms of this tautology are "what I want" (subject), "I want" (copula), and "when I want it" (predicate). "What I want" and "when I want it"—the what and when of want—are tautologous in their identities as desire.

Think before you think!
Stanislaw Lec

A philosophical aspect of tautology is expressed in a speech in Shakespeare's *Twelfth Night:*

As the old Hermit of Prague, that never saw pen and ink, very wittily said to a niece of King Gorboduc, "That that is is!"

To reformulate this subtle formulation: "That" (subject) "is" (copula) "that is" (predicate). "That" and "that is" are almost identical, but not quite.

Why is this thus? What is the reason of this thusness? (Artemus Ward)

Thus means "like this." So the first sentence can be rephrased "Why is this like this?", and the second, "What is the reason of this like-this-ness?" The terms of this tautology are subtly different; if only in the one different syllable between "this" and "thus," and in the meaning given by the order of the words, the role they play in the sentence.

A comment sometimes made on theaters of war is **Ah well, they say it's not as bad as they say it is.**

Here the terms are seemingly contradictory, but in the end are not, since the opposing terms come from the same source—"they" and their sayings.

A thing is worth whatever the buyer will pay for it. (Publilius Syrus)

Rephrase this as "the worth of a thing" (first term) "is" (copula)

<hr>

A bore is someone who, when you ask him how he is, tells you.

<hr>

"whatever the buyer will pay for it" (second term). Sometimes we forget that prices are arbitrary, that valuable things are free, and that expensive things are not always worthy. Publilius Syrus reminds us of the marketplace.

The satirical and sexy Roman poet Martial wrote:

You will always be poor, if you are poor, Aemianus.
Wealth is given today to none save the rich.

Wealth has usually been given to the rich by inheritance. The poor have to pull themselves up by their bootstraps.

There is a biblical echo in Shakespeare's

To gild refined gold, to paint the lily,
To throw a perfume on the violet.

This describes our efforts to improve on the perfect. (This is sometimes misquoted as "to gild the lily.")

I have been a stranger in a strange land. (Book of Exodus)

There is a splendid contrast here between the land perceived as strange by the protagonist and the way the protagonist is perceived by both himself and others in that land.

The terms of a tautology can differ considerably in emphasis.

The "Ancient Mariner" would not have taken so well if it had been called "The Old Sailor." (Samuel Butler)

Butler points out that the lofty speech of "Ancient Mariner" could be translated into the bathos of "Old Sailor."

That would be the most disastrous possible solution.
Charles de Gaulle

---

4. Visual TAUTOLOGY

In a visual tautology two similar terms are linked by a visual copula. My drawing *Déjà Vu* (2) shows the future, represented by the scene through the car window, and the past, represented by the scene reflected in the rearview mirror, as identical in appearance. The only difference between the terms is one of scale—the past seems smaller than the future. The present is perhaps represented by the thickness of the glass of the windshield and the mirror, an invisible thinness through which we perceive where we are going or have been. The small road (the past) is linked to the real road (the future) by the reflexivity of the mirror.

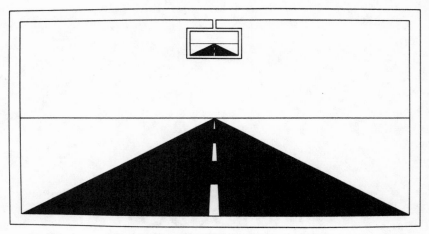

2. Déjà Vu
(Patrick Hughes)

René Magritte's *This Is a Piece of Cheese* (3) has two terms, painted cheese and real cheese, linked by the glass cheese cover. Magritte is alleging that a realistic painting of a piece of cheese, if it partook of real realism, would need to be kept fresh, that it could change as reality does and become stale or rotten.

Representation and reality are linked by this real copula, the cover. The frame around the painting is like the cover over the dish; it keeps in the reality.

3. This Is a Piece of Cheese
(René Magritte. Copyright © ADAGP, Paris, 1982.)

5. Verbal
OXYMORON

The opposite of the pleonasm is the oxymoron. In the pleonasm the adjective repeats the noun, in the oxymoron the adjective contradicts the noun. In a simile, Robert Burns said, "My love is like a red, red rose," finding qualities of beauty, color, and freshness in common between the love and the rose. Oxymoronically you go further, not to a comparison but to an antithesis, forcing the mind to run the gamut of an axis of meaning in seeking some vehemence of expression:

My wife has a whim of iron. (Oliver Herford)

This ploy is a poignant one. Iron and whim are poles apart. The hidden parallel with "a will of iron" shows that she is indeed a ruler. If her whim is so hard, what would her will be like?

Will and whim are opposites, as are, say, iron and feathers. A simile could be "My wife has whims like falling feathers"; like is compared with like. In oxymoron, like is compared with unlike, and the comparison, unlikely though it is, holds a wealth of meaning.

When it is said that the adjective contradicts the noun, it must be emphasized that these are deliberate oppositions along the same continuum. The terms in opposition are like themselves in that they are other, opposite aspects of the same thing. Milton's **No light, but rather darkness visible** contains the idea of visible darkness, darkness that can't be seen. But darkness and light are the furthest ends of the *same* spectrum; they are different aspects of visibility.

This theme in oxymoron is strong: Victor Hugo's last words in 1885 were **I see the black light!**

There is **black light** in the Professor's lecture in Lewis Carroll's *Sylvie and Bruno;* **darkness light** in Christian Morgenstern; and Samson's first soliloquy in Milton's *Samson Agonistes* includes the line **The sun to me is dark.**

In the Bible in the Book of Isaiah, chapter lvii, verse 10, we find **The darkness shall be as the noon-day.**

In attempting to define large areas, the oxymoron is useful because it sets up two poles of meaning between which the reader can fill in.

Music: cathedrals in sound. (Alfred Brumeau)

Brumeau, faced with the enormity of defining music, looks to the so solid and silent cathedrals for contrast with invisible sound. Construction and imagination and devotion are in common.

Architecture is frozen music. (Goethe)

Water is temporarily frozen, often in tremendous natural patterns and shapes, revealing mathematical structures, whereas music runs like water, never repeating itself exactly. Ice is quiet and is often perceived in, say, the silence of winter in the woods. Goethe's antithesis of frost and organized sound illuminates the permanent and decorative art of building. It is a magical idea that overnight a frost could still and silence music into monochromatic architecture.

Painting is silent poetry, poetry is painting that speaks. (Simonides of Ceos)

> If you have any friendship for me, be my enemy.
> William Blake

Simonides seems to be saying that poetry is more than painting; it is painting (which is silent) plus sound, whereas painting is like poetry but without the ingredient of sound. On the other hand, his oxymorons of silent poetry and speaking painting are poignant: if painting is silent poetry it is pure poetry—the essence, not the mere disturbance, of the airwaves. And painting that speaks, which we now have in the movies, must have seemed an unthinkably brilliant and lifelike achievement to the ancient Greeks.

God . . . a gaseous vertebrate. (Ernst Haeckel)

To define God is difficult. Haeckel compares his gassy nature—an ethereal thought in men's minds—with his vertebrate nature—a father-figure with a beard and robes who sits on a chair in the clouds. There is a hint of the guessing game "Animal, Vegetable, Mineral" here.

In seeking to describe people, those various and maddening folk, people have often resorted to the oxymoron. Oscar Wilde remarked of someone, **He hadn't a single redeeming vice.**

The usual phrase is "He hasn't a single redeeming virtue." In Wilde's oxymoron, redemption and vice, opposite ends of the scale of divine judgment, are yoked. The writer clearly felt that this was a person so frightfully virtuous that at least a single vice would make him more human.

I do not know upon what subject he will next employ his versatile incapacity. (A. E. Housman)

Housman's judgment is that for someone incapable a willingness to embark upon new subjects shows versatility but is obviously unproductive. Incapacity, a negative ability, is versatile in that it can be employed upon any subject with very poor results.

Christopher Hassall remarked of Dame Edith Sitwell: **She's genuinely bogus.** Hassall pits "genuine" against "bogus," complete antonyms. The implication is that there are other people who are bogus boguses, fraudulent frauds. Sitwell is a real fraud. She meant to be as consciously a poetess as she was; she did not hope to deceive others, though she may have been deceiving herself about the nature of the poet.

There is a form of verbal oxymoron where the verb contradicts its predicate, or the subject contradicts the verb:

Lawyers spend a great deal of their time shoveling smoke. (Oliver Wendell Holmes, Jr.)

You cannot shovel smoke, or at least it is very difficult. The verb "shovel" usually has something more tangible than smoke as its predicate.

If Greece has taught us that marble bleeds, Rome shows us that dust flowers. (Cecil Roberts)

All this relaxation has exhausted me.
Ashleigh Brilliant

The verb "bleeds" would not usually have "marble" as its subject. Marble breaks; it does not bleed. The meaning here is that the marble statuary of the Greeks was moving, tragic, could metaphorically bleed. The verb "flowers" is never used of "dust": dust is dead; flowering is life. "Dust flowers" is a way of saying "history speaks."

Those oxymorons in which verbs and other words are in great dissonance are often expressive of difficulty or resourcefulness:

For he a rope of sand could twist
As tough as learned Sorbonist. (Samuel Butler)

The last thing you could make a rope out of would be sand. There are a number of examples of futile expenditures of energy:

[It was like] **nailing jelly to the ceiling.**

[It was like] **carrying water in a sieve.**

To many people dramatic criticism must be like trying to tattoo soap bubbles. (John Mason Brown)

There are also oxymorons that describe difficult social occasions:

They agreed to differ. (Robert Southey)

He built castles in the air. (Robert Burton)

A silence you could cut with a knife. (Rabelais)

Extreme stupidity is elaborated by clever makers of oxymorons. Jokebooks contain stories about the fool who **applied for a job as a deckhand on a submarine;** and the fool who **was taking his**

I'd give my right arm to be ambidextrous.
Graffito

---

driving test—he rolled forward starting up a hill; and the fool who was given a pair of water skis for his birthday by his wife. Some months later when he still hadn't used them, she asked him why not, and he told her he couldn't find a lake with a slope.

The deckhand on the submarine is submerged—his is a bad job. The person who rolled forward up a hill was so foolish that he was not even influenced in his incapacity by gravity. A lake with a slope defies gravity.

"Who was it that called?"

"It was a gentleman, ma'am, looking for the wrong house."

"Finding the wrong house" and "looking for the right house" are here condensed into "looking for the wrong house." It is foolish to do so; yet he was looking and did arrive at the wrong house, so at least he looked at the wrong house as he tried to find the right house.

What are you doing with that piece of iron?

Trying to bend it straight.

When we bend things we usually think of bending them bent; the blacksmith in his work takes the meaning of bending as "adjusting the relative disposition of the parts" of the pieces of iron, including straightness. (Bending things takes them through any of the 360 degrees of planar geometry; straightness is an attribute only of 180 degrees.)

> Punctuality is the thief of time.
> Oscar Wilde

Extremes meet in the oxymoron:

Men's evil manners live in brass; their virtues we write in water. (William Shakespeare)

Writing—making marks on more or less permanent and solid surfaces—is extremely difficult to do on water, which is as far as possible from a permanent and solid surface. (John Keats chose "Here lies one whose name was writ in water" for the inscription on his tombstone.)

The chess player Viktor Korchnoi, failing in a match, remarked: **Well, I won one game in a row.** A row is more than one of a thing, lined up. But a row must start somewhere, with one. How short can a row be?

At the battle of Mobile, Alabama, in 1815, Andrew Jackson, later the seventh President of the United States, ordered: **Elevate those guns a little lower!** This malapropism is also an oxymoron, as elevate means "to raise up"—the gunners could not raise up lower. Jackson knew "elevate" had to do with the movement of the guns up and down, but he did not know at that moment (in battle) that its meaning is restricted to upward motion.

In the twentieth century, artists—especially the Surrealists—began to make contradictory objects, visual oxymorons, some of which are illustrated and analyzed in the next chapter. There have been many descriptions in words of objects which are contradictory, which could not exist, which would be useless. There is a category of *sleeveless errands* that new apprentices are required to run to fetch such objects, or they may be described and called for on April Fool's Day. They include:

steam pies
left-handed screwdrivers
square rings
sky hooks
straight hooks
hen's teeth
reels of tartan cotton
pigeon's milk
striped paint
stirrup oil
elbow grease

MORE ON
OXYMORON

a **balsa-wood anvil**

cooking glue

smooth sandpaper

I remember as a child being surprised to hear a color described as **sky-blue pink**.

Oxymoronic objects and people are also described in extravagant similes that seek to describe the ultimate:

It was as bad as being up the creek in a barbed wire canoe.

That is about as useful as a plastic frying pan.

He is about as useful as a one-armed paperhanger.

That's a lie—like a hairy egg.

That is as funny as a rubber crutch in a polio ward.

It was as hard as a brick banana (or **a concrete cucumber**).

That is as useful as a rubber dagger in a knife fight. (Barry Norman)

He was so black that charcoal would leave a white mark.

That is as rare as rocking-horse shit.

Sincere diplomacy is no more possible than dry water or wooden iron. (Joseph Stalin)

Stale bread is like a newly born fossil. (Ramon Gomez de la Serna)

The discontented child cries for toasted snow. (Arab proverb)

That's as useful as a chocolate teapot.

That went over like a lead balloon.

The **lead balloon** is reminiscent of the remark of G. C. Lichtenberg, eighteenth-century German aphorist and physicist, who, emphasizing the overdoing of a funeral, described **A bell of lead, to be rung during mourning.**

For the sake of completeness I list here some more oxymoronic epithets applied to people and their behavior. Some people

are born old

make deliberate mistakes

are compulsory volunteers

do things accidentally on purpose

are lazy bees

are straw dogs

are paper tigers

have happy accidents

keep open secrets

are the wisest fools

exercise their pork swords

chase iron butterflies

use dumb waiters

fear the mighty atom

mark the beginning of the end (Talleyrand)

The ancient writer Cicero seems to have been the first to refer to **a tempest in a teacup.** (He actually wrote something like "a billow in a basin.") This is an interesting oxymoron because it brings up the question of distinction of scale referred to in the section on visual pleonasm. The opposing terms "storm" and "teacup" differ enormously in size, not between material and thing, or by being different ends of the same continuum of meaning. On the other hand, if one bears in mind that the storm is presumably at sea, the sea and the contents of a teacup are both part of the continuum of liquids, though one is at the small end and one at the large end.

One use of verbal oxymoron is as a title. To call a book or a play by an oxymoronic title attempts to encompass the realm of the entire work within a very few words, which might spark the area between two opposing poles and suggest the vitality and breadth of the work in question. N. F. Simpson wrote plays called *A Resounding Tinkle* and *One-Way Pendulum.*

G. K. Chesterton wrote *Tremendous Trifles.*

Oliver Goldsmith wrote *She Stoops to Conquer.*

David Riesman wrote *The Lonely Crowd.*

The Lonely Crowd is an echo of a line from William Wordsworth's "The Quantocks":

> . . . these populous slopes
> With all their groves and with their murmurous woods,

Giving a curious feeling to the mind
Of **peopled solitude.**

Oxymoron is a figure much used in poetry. Unfortunately it is beyond the scope of this study to quote extensively from poetry. Here are just two lines:

Poverte is hateful good and, as I gesse . . . (Geoffrey Chaucer, "The Wife of Bath's Tale")

. . . the murderous innocence of the sea. (William Butler Yeats, "A Prayer for My Daughter")

Oxymoron meets mixed metaphor when the mixture is contradictory:

His shoes fit him like a glove.

We can say of many items of apparel that they fit like a glove, but shoes are at once too close to gloves—hands and feet are somewhat similar and too far apart; the use of shoes and the use of gloves seem very different. The distinctions are between softness and hardness, pliability and durability. (There is an echo here of René Magritte's famous painting *The Red Model*, in which the front halves of a pair of shoes take on the appearance of feet.)

William Gladstone, the English prime minister, once told a fellow Member of Parliament:

"Don't shake your head in the teeth of your own words."

I wouldn't be paranoid if people didn't pick on me.
Graffito

---

6. Visual
OXYMORON

In the visual version of oxymoron, the material of which a thing is made (or appears to be made) takes the place of the adjective, and the thing itself (or thing represented) takes the place of the noun. There is a difference between the verbal world and the visual world. The verbal world is entirely a construction of the human mentality; what I call the visual world includes pictures and sculptures, objects made of manufactured objects and other material, and natural things.

In the visual realm there are real things that are visual oxymorons untouched by man's hand (except in his perception). Consider the photograph (4) of sand, a sight often seen on beaches. These are waves made of sand. The essence of waves is their movement—here

4. Waves in the Sand
(photograph by Lawrence Lawry)

they are trapped in time. The essence of watery waves is their slippery translucent malleability—here they are stilled and solid. The action of the waves of water on the sand has been to create a visual oxymoron.

Trees are made of wood. The fossil tree (5) is a wooden tree that has come to be a stone tree. Stone is dead and cold and hard, while wood is alive and warm and softer. To my mind, one of the reasons we prize fossils—apart from the information they give us of growth gone by—is that they are oxymoronic. Living plants and animals are made by natural forces into their own contradictions. Stone lies at the other end of the scale to organic growth.

5. Tree in the Petrified Forest
(National Park Service)

The artist Anthony Earnshaw found half of a stone on heathland and noticed that it looked very much like half a loaf of bread. He put it on a breadboard with a knife (6). This is an oxymoron first of accident—the stone does by chance very much resemble bread in color and size and visual texture and shape; then of perception—Earnshaw saw this resemblance; and finally of design—the artist put the stone on the board with the knife in the bread context. The staff of life is at the other end of the spectrum of sustenance to stone.

Earnshaw calls the piece *Raider's Bread* and adds "the smash-and-grab raider eats a hearty breakfast before setting off to work."

6. Raider's Bread
(Anthony Earnshaw)

I have a childhood memory of construction sites where paper bags of concrete had been left to get wet and had solidified in the shape of the bag (7). Bags contain and conceal, can be used again and again, are adjustable to their contents and fold up; they are light and empty. This bag is just the reverse: it cannot contain or conceal, it shows itself, it is not adjustable or foldable, it is very heavy and entirely full. This accidental oxymoron makes the thing "bag" out of a diametrically opposed "concrete" material.

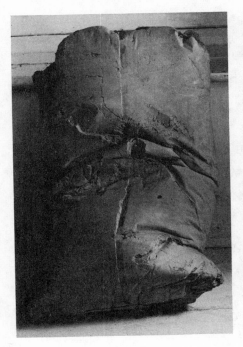

7. Concrete Bag
(photograph by Lawrence Lowry)

Sculpture, before the invention of abstract art, meant the representation of things in different materials. Sometimes transient materials such as ice or cheese or sand have been used. Topiary is a folk art, the trimming of hedges and bushes into the shape of things (8). An example is found in Chepstow, Wales: the ocean liner made of leaves and twigs, the ship that needs to be regularly cut back, opposes the massive opaque clanging structure of the real boat to the green, living, open leafy structure of the bush.

8. "The Queen Mary"
(Barnaby's Picture Library)

The usual material for sculpture has been stone, and the usual subject, people. The Mount Rushmore National Memorial (9) is a halfway house between stone and sculpture. The scale and nature of the mountain out of which the presidents have been made necessarily left the raw material showing. So we see rock people and rock itself. The scale of the men and their place at the top of the mountain make them like gods. Natural people are made of flesh and blood: soft, living, changing materials.

9. Mount Rushmore National Memorial
(Gutzon Borglum, photograph by Colin Macer)

The photograph of the sculptor at work (10) shows us a real man and a clay man. Later the clay man will be cast in plaster and then bronze. The real man will go away, grow old, and die; the bronze man will last forever.

Sculpture has to do with life and death. To make a person out of a more permanent material is to keep him alive longer. Madame Tussaud's waxworks museum in London, which began by recording the beheaded aristocracy of the French Revolution in wax, then the most lifelike, fleshy, and translucent substance available, is an attempt to defy death.

10. Sculptor and Model
(Wide World Photos)

There are some things that are radically changed in nature. One terrible change is death. In the case of human beings the material goes cold, stiff, green, rots, falls off. Plants wither, go brown, disappear. Perhaps a main motive for making visual oxymorons is the perception of these changes, and a desire to create something that denies the inevitable.

Cemeteries today are full of visual oxymorons on the subject of death (11). The ceramic everlasting flowers are meant to point up the fact of life blooming and then withering, while these flowers remain in bloom longer than human life.

11. Ceramic Flowers
(photograph by Lawrence Lawry)

The stone angel from the same cemetery in St. Ives, Cornwall, England (12), has stone wings that cannot fly.

12. Stone Angel
(photograph by Lawrence Lawry)!

This stone book in the cemetery (13), which lies forever open at the page of Alexander Taylor (1917–1959), denies the nature of books. Books are full of information in sequence, but this one denies us access to any other information. The open book is a closed book.

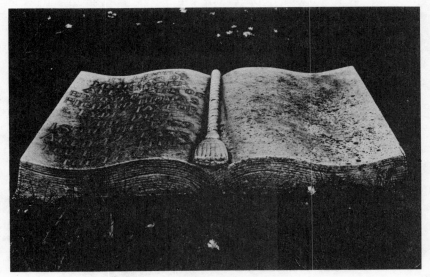

13. Stone Book
(photograph by Lawrence Lowry)

H. C. Westermann's *Jack* (14) is a jack o' lantern, which is usually made from a hollowed-out pumpkin; here it is made from a granite boulder. Pumpkin is pretty soft; granite is particularly hard. To quote the art critic Barbara Haskell: "He drew a face on it and took it to an old Connecticut tombstone carver to have the features sandblasted. He convinced the man to make it by telling him that a friend of his by the name of Jack Lantern, a member of the Hell's Angels, had been killed in a motorcycle accident and that he wanted to make a headstone for his grave."

14. Jack
(H. C. Westermann. Copyright
© H. C. Westermann, 1982.)

Ian Hamilton Finlay's *Marble Paper Boat* (15) takes the child's boat made of folded paper and re-presents it in marble, the hallowed stone of sculpture. Finlay's boat floats on a schematic sea of stone. In reality it would sink like a stone to the bottom of the pond. Some of the parameters in visual oxymoron are living and dead—the ceramic flowers, the fossil log, the liner made of leaves. This theme of lightness and weight is another.

15. Marble Paper Boat
(Ian Hamilton Finlay)

In a scene in Buster Keaton's film *The Boat,* Keaton throws his anchor overboard into the sea and it floats. Tony Blundell has drawn the scene (16). In the same movie Keaton throws a lifebelt into the sea and it sinks. This is not so potent a scene, as you somehow expect a lifebelt to sink. Lots of things sink; to our disappointment, few things float. There is a carved stone lifebelt in the churchyard of St. Ives, a fishing village.

In Keaton's anchor scene, part of the fun lies in the play between appearance and reality—the anchor looks like an anchor, but it performs like a lifebelt.

16. Buster Keaton's Anchor
(Tony Blundell)

Marcel Duchamp's *Why Not Sneeze, Rose Selavy?* (17) is a small birdcage filled with what appear to be sugar cubes. Duchamp noticed that sugar cubes resemble marble, and he had marble cut and finished to the same size and texture as sugar. The handle invites the viewer to feel the difference between what he sees as sugar and lifts as marble. Duchamp called this piece a "visual pun"; I think it is a visual illusion and an oxymoron.

17. Why Not Sneeze, Rose Selavy?
(Marcel Duchamp. Philadelphia Museum of Art:
The Louise and Walter Arensberg Collection.)

The joke sugar lumps (18) are a contemporary novelty made of plastic foam. Defying gravity, they float on the surface of the hot drink. Duchamp's sugar is heavier than sugar; this sugar is lighter than sugar.

18. floating Sugar
(photograph by Lawrence Lawry)

A further theme in visual oxymoron is rigidity and softness. A practical joke (19) is to give someone a rubber pencil when he or she wants to make a note of something. The pencil bends in the hand as it presses on the paper. Expectations are dashed. You feel a fool with this limp pencil.

19. Rubber Pencil
(photograph by Lawrence Lawry)

A magician sometimes invites children to step up onstage and hold the wand with which he has been making magic (20). To the consternation of the child, the wand falls limp (21). The author himself experienced this as a child.

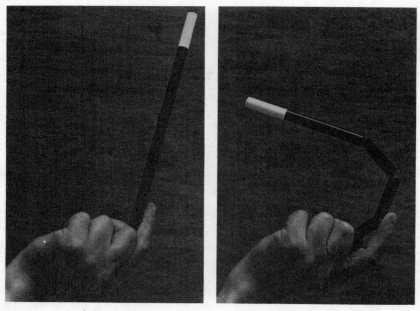

20. Magic Wand
(photograph by Lawrence Lowry)

21. Limp Magic Wand
(photograph by Lawrence Lowry)

This antithesis between soft and hard materials must be informed by our childish perception of our own bodies and those of others. Parents have hard and soft bits, and we have flesh and bone and muscle. Perhaps the seemingly magical erection and detumescence of the male member is also perceived as this antithesis. Salvador Dali's *The Persistence of Memory* (22) depicts soft watches. The structured, firm, regular nature of the object is contradicted by the sloppy, drooping, limp quality of the material. It has been said he was inspired by the sight of children's sugar watches in a candy-store window.

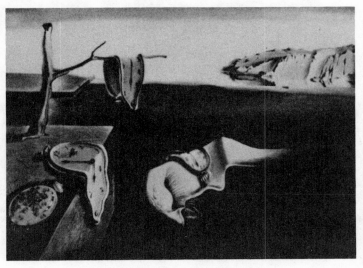

22. The Persistence of Memory
(Salvador Dali)

The American sculptor Claes Oldenburg has made a number of sculptures in vinyl and kapok, using the technology of the soft toy, which repeat Dali's image in three dimensions.

His *Ghost Drum Set* (23) lies limp, with limp cymbals, limp drumsticks, limp skins. Oldenburg has spoken of his sculpture as being like his body. Oldenburg's other "soft machines" include a soft typewriter, soft scissors, a soft toilet, and a soft telephone.

23. Ghost Drum Set
(Claes Oldenburg)

Hans Bellmer's *Corset-Bastille* (24) is an oxymoron on the theme of rigidity and undulation. Bricks, usually of the same size and laid out in regular rows, are drawn here in lines as sensually concave and convex as a human body. The hard and unyielding bricks represent an abstract shapely fleshiness. The material is brick; the thing, by implication, flesh.

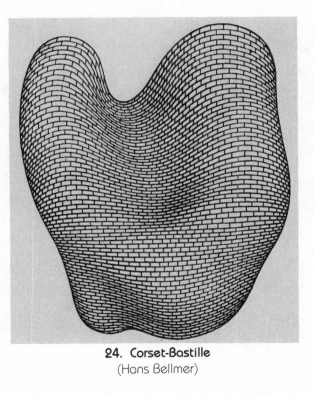

24. Corset-Bastille
(Hans Bellmer)

Liquids are runny. A gag from the joke shop is the spilled ink (25). The first meaning of this is to frighten a mother with the thought that you have spilled your ink on her tablecloth, then relieve her by picking it up.

As an object it is oxymoronic—it is a solid puddle, liquid you can pick up in one piece.

25. Spilled Ink
(photograph by Lawrence Lawry)

Man Ray's *What We All Lack* (26) is an object that also presents liquid as a solid. He took a bubble pipe and stuck a Christmas ball on the bowl. Instead of a transitory bubble, we have a permanent bauble. Both bubble and bauble are made by inflating a drop of liquid; the difference is that soapy water bursts, whereas glass keeps its globular shape forever. Ray's piece memorializes the moment of childish joy.

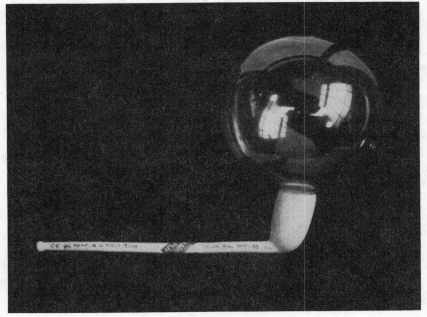

26. What We All Lack
(Man Ray)

Patrick Hughes's *On Reflection: St. Ives Bay* (27) takes the illusory to be real. The reflections of the toy boats are as real as the boats: they are the same boats from the same toyshop. This is a fifth theme in oxymoron: real illusion.

27. On Reflection: St. Ives Bay
(Patrick Hughes)

We have discussed real things, pictures of things, sculptures of things, things made into sculpture, and joke things. There is something inherently oxymoronic about visual representation: it is the attempt to pin down life. Life moves on, and the representation remains, a quixotic reminder of the difficulty of description.

The photograph of waves (28) keeps the water, which fell some years ago, in the air for as long as the pigment and paper last. The momentary is clothed in the permanent.

28. Photograph of Waves
(photograph by Lawrence Lawry)

Oxymoronic objects include:
plastic lemons
electric candles
rubber bones for dogs
floating soap
china eggs to persuade hens to lay
solid water (ice)
bricked-up windows
artificial grass
wax fruit
plastic flowers
invisible ink
glass hammers
a child's printed watch
a mirror used as a display lake
glass eyes
joke rubber coat hooks
false teeth and gums
iron ships
John Bunyan's iron fiddle
solid wooden bottle molds

It is reported that during the Second World War the Royal Air Force bombed dummy airplanes on a German airfield with wooden bombs.

7. Verbal
CONTRADICTION IN TERMS

The principal distinctions between the contradiction in terms and the oxymoron are that in the contradiction in terms we do not simply have a noun contradicted by its adjective but two opposing terms linked by a copula—an inactive verb such as "be" or "seem"— and that the terms are not used as poetically and vaguely as in the oxymoron, but with a more precise meaning, a more obvious opposition. In *Upon the Pun: Dual Meaning in Words and Pictures*, which I wrote with Paul Hammond, a similar distinction was made between the pun and the play on words: the pun has an irrational, playful quality, and the play on words has a rational, discursive nature.

The most incomprehensible thing about the world is that it is comprehensible. (Albert Einstein)

The terms "incomprehensible" and "comprehensible" are contradictory, and linked by "is." Each can apply to "the world" and our understanding of it. Einstein is saying how remarkable he finds it that physical laws are to be discovered and found to apply to a great range of phenomena. In that sense "incomprehensible" is being misused, since Einstein does understand that the world is comprehensible. He is just puzzled by why that is. Does it imply a God or some moving spirit? Could there be other worlds that we would not comprehend?

Robert Zend's remark **People have one thing in common: they are all different** has it that the terms "they are all different" and "[they] have one thing in common" can both be applied to "people." These terms are apparently contradictory, but the thing they have in common is their difference.

The fabricator of a contradiction in terms notices that however surely or vehemently you feel that a thing has such-and-such an attribute, you can often argue the opposite case as the devil's advocate.

She is intolerable, but that is her only fault. (Talleyrand, of a young lady of the court)

She has only one fault, but that fault is that she is intolerable: to have only one fault is to be virtually faultless, but to have the fault of being intolerable is the worst. This is a clever picture—the girl is wonderful but insufferable. Some people are.

Martial's tautology "Wealth is given today to none save the rich" is echoed in Oscar Wilde's **I should fancy that the real tragedy of the poor is that they can afford nothing but self-denial.**

"Real" is the clue that we are going to be given some new information. We might then expect, after "they can afford nothing but," something like "cheap food, which is not sustaining"; but Wilde gives us "self-denial." To deny oneself is the privilege of those who have some means to buy something; the poor can only work and search. Wilde was a socialist, and this is his way of criticizing the hypocrisy of the Victorian ruling classes. He has discovered a contradiction in that Christian attitude that suggests self-denial to the poor. (That is all they can do, he says: deny themselves the things, perhaps essential, that they cannot afford.)

Stanislaw Lec has written **Sometimes you have to be silent to be heard** and G. K. Chesterton said **Silence is the unbearable repartee.**

Silent is heard, and silence is repartee. These terms are apparently contradictory. Lec's meaning is that talking and shouting can be less effective, if it is the norm, than a more notable silence like Milton's "loud silence." Chesterton reminds us of some of the arguments we have had, and how effective and eloquent a rejoinder silence can be.

Uninvited guests are often most welcome after they have left. (William Shakespeare)

The terms "most welcome" and "after they have left" are contradictory. The absence of the uninvited guests is welcome, rather than the guests themselves.

A newspaper headline is said to have read **ASSASSIN TO BE TRIED!** If the defendant is to be tried, we do not know if he is an assassin yet; that still has to be decided by the court.

It usually takes more than three weeks to prepare a good impromptu speech. (Mark Twain)

Twain points up the way in which the impromptu speech is valued as evidence of the performer's ready wit and sincerity. Mark

Twain was a popular lecturer and knew how difficult it was to prepare speeches that appeared to be improvised.

Definition is to confine one term within the confines of another.

Stability itself is nothing else than a more sluggish motion. (Montaigne)

"Stability" is "motion," says Montaigne, because he believes everything is in flux, and that what we see as stability is only perceived as stability because we haven't the means to perceive the motion. So to define the world or parts of it as stable is too confining. We must see that it is in motion and hidden motion.

How do you get a fool confused? Put him in a barrel and tell him to stand in a corner.

By definition, a barrel does not have corners. To speak of the corner of a barrel is like talking of a square circle.

When Sir John Scott introduced into the British Parliament his bill for restraining the liberty of the press, a Member of Parliament moved as an additional clause that **all anonymous works should have the name of the author printed on the title page.** At that moment they would cease to be anonymous works. Perhaps the Member in his excitement had forgotten what "anonymous" means. "Anonymous" and "named" are antonyms.

Sir Boyle Roche, the eighteenth-century Irish maker of bulls,

> Death is nature's way of telling you to slow down.

speaking in favor of the union with Britain, said that one of its effects would be **"that the barren hills would become fertile valleys."** (This can be compared with Lewis Carroll's **"When you say 'hill,' the Queen interrupted, "I could show you hills, in comparison with which you'd call that a valley."**)

The definitions of "hill" and "valley" are mutually exclusive; even union with Britain could not change their essential nature. The terms are contradictory. It is said that Boyle Roche wrote these bulls before repeating them in the debating chamber.

When one has good health, it is not serious to be ill. (Francis Blanche)

We can think of this in one of two ways: either Blanche is a silly person who does not see that if you are ill you no longer have good health; or that if you are healthy in general, a particular bout of illness is not so serious.

Death is such an absolute and concern of the living that there are many jokes made about it. Life and death are contradictory terms.

> Is there a life before death?
> Belfast graffito

> The first condition of immortality is death.
> Stanislaw Lec

A man, learning that his nephew was going to become a priest, said to him, "I hope to live long enough to hear you preach my funeral oration!"

Another version is:

Said Jones to Smith: "I'd die happy if I could only live to see my own funeral."

What we are witnessing here is the will to live in the face of death.

Mark Twain once sent a cablegram from London to a New York newspaper:

The report of my death was an exaggeration.

Death is an absolute, incapable of exaggeration; such terms can never be in agreement. Twain is playing with the idea that the report exaggerated some news of an incapacity of his into the ultimate incapacity.

Often it is fatal to live too long. (Racine)

There is a play on the word "fatal" here, as it is being used both literally, meaning "dead" (as in a "fatal accident"), and metaphorically, meaning destructive of one's career as an artist (such that one might outlive one's success and become unfashionable).

The Belgian artist Marcel Mariën, five of whose works are

reproduced in this book, is also an aphorist. He coined the remark, in his book *Crystal Blinkers*, **As famous as the Unknown Soldier.**

The Unknown Soldier is a poignant institution in all the belligerent countries of the First World War. One of the dead and unidentified soldiers was taken and buried and celebrated as standing for the many who are dead and unidentified. He is famous. But what is his fame to him? Not only is he dead, he is unknown. "Famous" and "unknown" are contradictory terms.

"Strategy," answered the silly soldier to a selection board, "is when you don't let the enemy discover that you're out of ammunition by keeping on firing."

This bluff pits "keeping on firing" against "out of ammunition." What the silly soldier means is that there might be a little ammunition left that one should use, rather than remain silent and be defeated.

Our troops advanced today without losing a foot of ground. (War communiqué)

The true facts are sometimes hard to ascertain: either the troops advanced, they stayed where they were, or they fell back. We are in the realm of exaggeration. You can't lose a foot of ground when you advance.

I must follow the people. Am I not their leader? (Benjamin Disraeli)

Rephrased, this reads "the leader follows the people" instead of the conventional "the people follow the leader." This is like a chiasmus in that the usual order of the phrase is reversed. Similarly:

He led his regiment from behind. (W. S. Gilbert)

To lead from behind is to follow, or, to subtly urge forward.

Anarchists like **Don't vote. The government will get in.**

Many people have noticed how power corrupts. The argument is that once any party, no matter how idealistic, gets into power, it will be constrained by the realities of office. This could be rephrased "the opposition will become the government."

In the contradiction in terms, the ordinary point of view is undermined by making contradictory terms marry. It is a logical extension of the poetic and playful oxymoron.

"Come on, Joe. Climb up the searchlight for us."

"Do you take me for a fool? I know that trick."

"What trick?"

"When I'd be halfway up the light, you'd switch it off."

This theme is continued in the visual contradiction in terms.

8. Visual
CONTRADICTION IN TERMS

In a visual oxymoron, a thing is clothed in a contradictory material, the thing and its material having no particular meaning. On the other hand, in the visual contradiction in terms, the thing or its clothing will have meaning, and there will be a link comparable to the copula in the verbal contradiction in terms.

Light and darkness have long had a weight of meaning. The author's drawing *Darkness Falls* (29) has darkness, the absence of light, made visible as a thing. It falls as though it had weight, and it takes its shape from the window it comes through. Darkness is treated as a thing like, say, cake icing, which might take its shape from the tip of a pastry tube. Light is not a thing but energy in wave form. The window frame is the link between darkness and thing-ness.

29. Darkness Falls
(Patrick Hughes)

30. Re-found Object
(Marcel Mariën)

In terms of comfort, Marcel Mariën's *Re-found Object* (30) is a contradiction in terms. Sometimes stools have handles, which are holes cut into the middle of the seat. This one is an unhandy handle. It comforts in that it is an aid to carrying the stool, but it is uncomfortable to sit on. To replace a hole with something that sticks up, while retaining the meaning "handle," is Mariën's witty contradiction.

In John Heartfield's *"O Christmas Tree in a German Room, How Crooked Your Branches Are"* (31), the Christmas tree, symbol of the birth of Jesus (who loved us all), is couched in the terms of the swastika, symbol of the Nazi movement (known for its narrow love of the Aryan race). Each term has a strong meaning, and the two are linked in the shape of the tree.

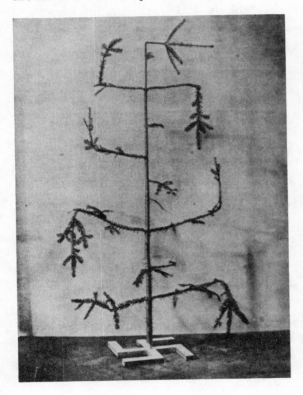

31. "O Christmas Tree in a German Room, How Crooked Your Branches Are" (John Heartfield)

In the record cover *Persecution and Mass Murder* (32), the terms barbed wire and Star of David are contradictory. The Star of David, signifying Jewish religious observance, is couched in barbed wire, which has come to symbolize the concentration camps in which the Nazis killed Jews. A Star of David would normally be made of precious metal, not barbed wire. Barbed wire, if it has a shape, is in rolls or lines. The malleability of the barbed wire links Jews and concentration camps.

32. Persecution and Mass Murder
(Falk/Bergentz/Lenskog)

René Magritte's *Drawing* (33) is of a candle that gives forth darkness. The darkness diminishes with its distance from the flame, just as light does. The woman's face is illuminated in reverse; she becomes visible as her distance from the light increases. This is a visual equivalent of Milton's oxymoron "darkness visible." The terms that are contradictory here are light and darkness, and the link is the candle. Magritte is saying that things cannot be seen by their light alone, that the dark parts are necessary to see the vision, too. Perhaps the photographic negative is a source of the thought behind this work.

33. Drawing
(René Magritte. Copyright © ADAGP, Paris, 1982.)

Anthony Earnshaw's *Snowman on a Bonfire* (34) conflates two terms, one English and one universal. On November 5 English children burn an effigy of Guy Fawkes, who attempted to blow up Parliament in the seventeenth century. In wintertime children make men of snow. This combination is not inflammatory: the snowman will melt and douse his flames. He will cease to exist and so will the fire: stalemate. Earnshaw notes "he wears a scarf and a hat to keep warm, and holds a broom to beat out the flames." The terms "flammable" and "inflammable" are linked by the childish effigies.

34. Snowman on a Bonfire
(Anthony Earnshaw)

Saul Steinberg's *Cube* (35) is posed in two terms, abstract geometry and the real life of things. The way in which things decay, crack, grow weeds, are patched up, suffer the elements, age, is pitted against the clear visual argument of a Platonic solid ABCDEF(G)H. The contradictory terms "ideal" and "real" are linked in the cube.

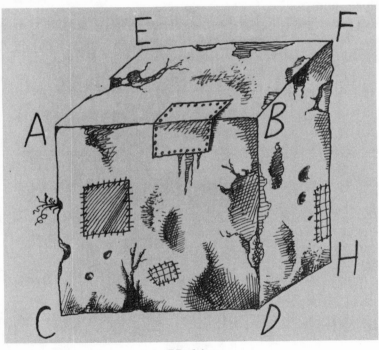

35. Cube
(Copyright © Saul Steinberg, 1960)

As the poem suggests, the oval wheels of Gelett Burgess (36) will not give regular movement. Burgess's wheels draw our attention to the difference between reality and our perception of it. The wheels in pictures after the invention of perspective are oval to accord with our perceptions rather than our conceptions. The camera's perception of circles as ovals joins the contradictory terms "ellipse" and "wheel."

In times gone by, apprentice wheelwrights made wooden oval wheels to demonstrate their skill. The surrealist André Breton had one in his collection.

36. Elliptical Wheels
(Gelett Burgess)

Remarkable
    Truly is Art!
See — Elliptical
    Wheels on a Cart!
It Looks Very Fair
In the Picture, up There,
But Imagine the
    Ride, when you Start!

9. Verbal
OBVIOUS

The field next to the field of tautology is the field of the obvious. The word "obvious" comes from the Latin *ob*, meaning "in the way of," and *viam*, meaning "the way." Thus it translates as "in the way of the way." If in a tautology the two linked terms are different words for the same meaning (e.g., "When large numbers of men are unable to find work, unemployment results"), in the obvious the relationship between the two terms will be one not so much of identity as of intrinsic meaning.

A young army cadet was attending a selection board.

"Well," said a ribbon-bedecked general, "what must an officer be before he can have a funeral with full military honors?"

"Dead," answered the cadet.

The answer was given in the question. Obviously the simple boy was profound; he ignored the question as to what rank the officer would have to be, and answered the life-or-death question.

A commercial traveler was passing through a small town when he saw a sumptuous funeral going past.

"Who's died?" he asked a passer-by.

"I'm not sure," replied the local, "but I think it's the one in the hearse."

The "who" of the person in the coffin is taken for the "who" of all the people in the procession, including the one in the coffin. It is obvious that the dead person is the one in the hearse.

The saddest moment in a person's life comes only once. (Brendan Francis)

Of the various sad moments, one of them is the saddest. But until the life is over, one is not in a position to review the life to decide. This remark is some kind of consolation: there is only one saddest moment, though there may be lots of sad moments.

The more one has lived, the less it remains to us to live. (J. Pons Viernet)

This is a slippery conceit. It is as if the length of the life can be known before it ends. If you've so far lived twelve days, then indeed there may only be seventy-four years and a hundred and ten days

---

Dark windows are often a very clear proof.
Stanislaw Lec

> The dumplings in a dream are not dumplings, but dreams.

left of that life, but that does not mean much to a babe in arms. It has a different meaning if you have lived hard, and you are fifty-four, and you can dimly perceive an end to life.

"He lived his life to the end." (Anonymous)

Indeed he did. So do all of us. There is another meaning, that he lived his life *fully* to the end. He lived life rather than merely existed. There is a latent absurdity here, that one might not live one's life to the end, but live it to some indeterminate point and then stop.

No wonder I feel so tired—I'm older now than I've ever been before. (Ashleigh Brilliant)

Brilliant's remark is obvious, true of all of us, yet not often remarked upon. Of course it does not govern how tired we feel; that might vary from day to day.

You always find something the last place you look.

One implication is that "the last place you look" is a particular place, that it is somewhere you might look sooner and avoid the delay. This is slippery. And if you looked there sooner, and found what you were after, it would *still* be the *last place you looked*! This makes it a little like the Surprise Inspection paradox described in the author's *Vicious Circles and Infinity*. Another stoic aspect is that the object *will* be found, if it is found, at the end of the search.

We are tomorrow's past. (Mary Webb)

Webb's remark brings together three periods of time—the past, the present, and the future—in the words "are," "tomorrow's," and "past." It is a way of saying the future has a past. It is at once profound and silly—profoundly silly. It is obvious in that these terms are to some extent interchangeable: the future can become the present and the past; the present can become the past; and the past remains the past.

The weather had been very bad, and the blizzard disrupted the traffic all around. Buses were snowbound, and cars found difficulty in traveling, when a telegram arrived for the manager of the department store from his floor supervisor, Henderson. *Will not be in office today. Haven't arrived home yesterday yet—Henderson.*

He believes that yesterday is a day that includes getting home, as usual. His day will not be complete until he gets home.

The way in which things work is a source of the obvious. The permanent way is in the way of being a way:

The tourist found himself at the railway station and thought he would make conversation with the old porter. "Tell me," he asked, "where does this railway line go?"

"Nowhere. It's been in the one place all my life."

Lost, as water is lost in water.
Jorge Luis Borges

In part this is a deception; it is not the line that goes, it is the trains thereon. On the other hand, it does clearly lead to at least one other place.

Similarly, **A simpleton was once asked why they built the railway station two miles from the town.**

He answered: "Well, they thought it would be a good idea to have the station near the railway."

He is answering another question: not "Why isn't the station nearer the town?" but "Why is the station near the tracks?" (which are two miles out of town). We might ask how and why each was built where it separately was.

The visitor complained of the long muddy avenue to the hotel.

"Well now," soothed the proprietor, "if it was any shorter it wouldn't reach the house."

The proprietor, considering the two qualities of his avenue, ignores its muddiness and takes up its length: it is exactly the right length to reach the house. It is unlikely that anyone would have a driveway to a house that does not reach the house. Much worse than it being long and muddy for it not to reach there at all.

A group of men were discussing Stephen Douglas and his physical peculiarities. Abraham Lincoln happened to join the men at

---

The noblest prospect which a Scotchman ever sees
is the highway to England.
Johnson

---

this point and, turning from the specific subject under discussion, one of them asked the President how long he thought a man's legs should be.

"Well," drawled Lincoln, "I should think a man's legs ought to be long enough to reach from his body to the ground."

The legs might also be said to reach from the ground to his body. Certainly legs have to be in touch with both body and ground most of the time. Legs too short to reach to the ground are not possible. Whatever length one's legs are, they do the job of keeping one in contact with the ground.

Did you hear about the silly man who told his mother he was glad she'd named him Bill because everybody calls him by that name?

Reversed, this reads "everybody calls him by that name because she had named him Bill." He is called Bill because of her naming; he thinks it a happy accident that his Bill-self fits with the name everyone calls him.

Thank God for water. If there was no water we wouldn't be able to learn how to swim, and then we'd all drown.

"There was no water" soon turns into "we'd all drown."

Tact consists in knowing how far to go too far.
Jean Cocteau

Leo Rosten quotes a Jewish "prayer":

Dear God: I know you will provide, but why don't you provide *until* you provide?

This is about the relation between the future and the present; the person praying wants the future now. But when does the future start? Is it not awful the way it keeps getting put off?

10. Visual
OBVIOUS

Marcel Mariën's drawing *Intimacy* (37) shows a new relation. Instead of the shoe fitting the foot, the foot fits the shoe. The foot extends itself to fit into the high heel of the shoe. The contained fits the container. Mariën is joking along the lines of "If women look like this in high heels, would they look like this out of high heels?"

In Murray McDonald's *Wheeled Line* (38) the wheels that usually cause engines and trucks to travel along the stationary line instead enable the line itself to travel. The way is open for the line to make its way about the world. Will it travel past the trains as they travel over it, or will it go one way and the trains another?

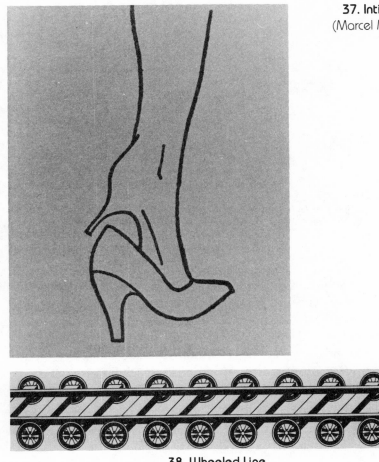

37. Intimacy
(Marcel Mariën)

38. Wheeled Line
(Murray McDonald)

11. Verbal
FIGURE/GROUND REVERSAL

The Gestalt school of psychologists—Koffka, Kohler, Wertheimer—sought to emphasize the relation in perception between figure and ground. The figure, they said, tended to be more prominent, symmetrical, simple, and organized. The ground, by comparison, would be found disorganized, asymmetrical, and so on. The picture *The Hidden Heads* (39) shows a situation in which figure can become ground and ground figure. The Gestalt psychologists argued that one could perceive either the vase or the heads outlined at each side of it, but not both at the same time. Each could take its turn being the figure, each the ground. (There are a number of other hidden heads.)

To reiterate: in the oxymoron there is wild opposition; in pleon-

39. The Hidden Heads (Eighteenth Century)

> Sometimes the bell swings the bellman.
> Stanislaw Lec

asm, tautology, and the obvious, things are in very close relation; in the contradiction in terms, things are carefully and conscientiously opposed. In the figure/ground reversal the usual disposition is transposed.

Thou has been considering whether the chicken came first from the egg or the egg from the chicken. (Macrobius, c. 400 A.D.)

One can put the cart before the horse, see the situation from the other side, turn something upside down, inside out, the other way around.

Lewis Carroll, who loved inversions and mirror images, gave a piece of advice to the letter-writer: lick the envelope, not the stamp. That way you do not lick the glue off the stamp, you do not get the glue on your taste buds, you do not have to lick exactly to the corners. It works.

"Hey, Bill, you're wearing odd socks!"

"You're right! Both of them!"

What is odd is the relation between them, that they are different in color. Each of them is different from the other; they share that difference.

A man was sitting in a pub wearing one blue sock and one red sock.

"That's a strange pair of socks you've got on," said a friend.

Those who live in stone houses should not throw glass.

"Yes, it is," he replied. "And do you know, I've got another pair at home just like it."

Two pairs of socks—a red sock and a blue sock, and a blue sock and a red sock—could become two regular pairs. But the silly man sees the temporary entity of the socks he is wearing, one blue and one red, as an absolute pair, a figure to be seen against the ground of the other pair. He does not see the four socks as an entity to be made into two single-colored pairs.

"It's a strange thing," he said, "But I've never seen a man with one short leg but the other was longer."

If a man has a short leg, then the other one—the normal-size one—will necessarily be longer. If the short one is seen as the figure against the longer and thus called shorter, to see the longer against the figure of the shorter and thus call it longer is to alternate the figure/ground relationship.

A drunken sailor was asked why he was walking with one foot on the pavement and the other in the gutter.

"Is that what I'm doing?" he replied. "Thank heaven! I thought I was a cripple."

There is a syllogism here: I am hobbling. Cripples hobble. Therefore I am a cripple.

But there are reasons for hobbling other than being a cripple.

One ground against which one would see one's legs as a figure is the pavement; if one makes the ground two different heights by walking with one foot in the gutter and fails to perceive that, the legs will appear to be of different lengths against a presumed flat ground.

A woman met a man limping along the road wearing only one shoe.

"What's up?" she asked. "Lost a shoe?"

"No," replied the man. "Just found one!"

The situation of only having one shoe is usually seen against the background of having had two and lost one. Here the situation is reversed and presumes a barefoot person finding a shoe and putting it on. It is more convenient to be barefoot than one-shoed.

"Jones," said the sergeant sarcastically, "do you know the rest of the platoon is out of step except you."

"You'd better tell them, Sergeant. You're in charge."

The sergeant's irony calls attention to the other possibility. In, say, political morality, or avant-garde art, the rest could be out of step with the prophet. But in a marching platoon the majority is the figure, and the sole person out of step is the ground. There is a scene in which a leader, having called for volunteers to take one pace forward while his back is turned, turns around to find the

---

Down with gravity.
Graffito

---

platoon still in one line. This is because they have all silently stepped forward one pace.

SMALL AD: For sale. Man's suit. Perfect fit.

Fit for whom? It obviously fits the person who used to wear it (probably the same person who is selling it), but what can we know of its fit on the person invited to buy it? A perfect fit must be seen as a figure/ground relationship, in which the figure fits exactly into the ground of the suit. Here the suit is a ground already announced as a perfect fit for an unknown figure.

Customer buying a tie: "Can I bring it back if it doesn't fit me?"

Ties fit everyone. Once I sold ties in a street market. My sales pitch was **"Adjustable ties! Get your adjustable ties here!"**

The story is told of **the silly identical twins who couldn't tell each other apart.** For other people, either one of the two figures might easily be too similar to the other one to be perceived as different, for one to be the figure and the other the ground. But it is extremely unlikely for one twin not to perceive the other as different from himself. It might be that other people could not tell them apart, but they *are* apart.

Conrad and James were trying to get a mule into the barn, but its ears were too long.

"Wait," said Conrad, "let's raise the barn."

"No," said James. "Why don't we dig a trench?"

"No, you dummy," yelled Conrad. "It's the ears that are too long, not the legs."

Ears, legs, roof, floor are the possibilities. (The fact that the ears are easily bent down is an extra joke.) Because the ears are too

> The professional arsonist builds vacant lots for money.
> Jimmy Breslin

long, the barn must be raised; since the legs are not too long, a trench must not be dug. Conrad perceives the ears as a figure, fails to perceive the whole mule as a figure, and fails to perceive the relative height of the barn door as a figure against the ground of the mule's overall height.

It takes a hundred fools to put a screw in a wall. One to hold the screw—and the other ninety-nine to turn the wall.

Is the screw to be the figure, and the wall the ground, or vice versa? Here the fools notice that often operations can be performed the other way around (compare *The Haunted Swing* in the visual section).

Michael and Todd were nailing up the side of a wooden bungalow. Todd noticed that Michael was examining the nails and throwing away every second or third.

"What's wrong with the nails?" he asked.

"The heads are on the wrong end."

"You idiot, they're for the other side of the house!"

The chance way in which Michael picked up the nails, head first or tail first, does not determine their usefulness. The head is not on the wrong end; Michael has hold—momentarily—of the wrong end. This situation can be adjusted. That the "wrong-ended" nails are for the other side of the house compounds the wish to perceive the world of nails as of right nails against wrong nails, a figure/ground situation, rather than a reversible system.

An Englishman being driven through Dublin by a taxi driver asked as they passed a big building, "What is that fine place?"

"Oh, sir," came the reply, "that's the post office—but you should see the front. This is only the back—the front's behind."

The figure/ground relationship exists in the front/behind dichotomy. Where the front is behind, we are shown the relativity of these judgments, the possibility of instant reversal.

A detective arrested a criminal and was about to handcuff him when a huge gust of wind blew the detective's hat off.

"Shall I go and fetch it?" the prisoner asked.

"Do you take me for a fool?" asked the detective. "You wait here while I go and get it!"

The detective takes "here" and "there" as constants, as places rather than as relative positions. If the detective and his prisoner are parted, it does not much matter where they are, here or there. Here is not better than there for a detective if the prisoner is not here.

Irreligion: the principal one of the great faiths of the world.

Ambrose Bierce

"Hammond, do you plead guilty?"

"I couldn't say, your Honor. I haven't heard the evidence yet."

Hammond is treating the court like an episode of a TV series rather than as a means of discovering the truth about his activities. The figure is his past activities as reflected in his plea, and the ground is the evidence. Hammond reverses the relationship and bases his view of the past on the evidence yet to come.

Aside from the popular jokes cited above, literary aphorists and wits have emphasized the possibility of viewing the conventional figure/ground relationship as reversible.

We see things not as they are, but as we are. (H. M. Tomlinson)

Our perception—and figure/ground relationships are a matter of perception—is two-way. We think of things as they are, but Tomlinson reminds us to remember that we are, too, and that we see what we are predisposed to see.

Things do not change, we do. (Henry David Thoreau)

Thoreau has noticed how we have remarked on things changing, and he draws our attention to the equally likely other possibility that our perception of them has changed as we have ourselves changed.

Do not adjust your mind, there is a fault in reality. (Graffito in Brighton, U.K.)

This is a version of "Do not adjust your TV set, there is a fault in the transmission." It is saying: "Maybe it is not your fault; maybe there is something rotten in the state of Denmark."

It is well to remember, my son, that the entire population of the universe, with one trifling exception, is composed of others. (John Andrew Holmes)

Most often we see the rest of the world as ground to our figure. Holmes wittily places the entire population of the universe, composed of others, against each of us: the one trifling exception. A salutary reminder of the one-sidedness of solipsism.

'Tis the same to him who wears a shoe, as if the whole earth were covered with leather. (Ralph Waldo Emerson)

Our mediocre perception of the situation is that a foot wears a shoe that protects it, occludes its perceptions from and of the earth. Emerson collects all the footsteps and sees them as covering the whole earth with leather, like a football. Barefoot on a leather ball, rather than feeling the world through the sole.

The would-be wit found himself put down when, at the dinner table, he held up his fork with a piece of meat on it and asked his hostess, "Is this pig?"

"To which end of the fork do you refer?" asked one of his fellow guests.

The picture is of a man, a fork, and a piece of meat, interconnected. For the man holding the fork, the figure is the meat on the pronged end of the fork; the other guest turns it around to suggest there is a pig on the handle end.

"Won't you come into the garden? I would like my roses to see you." (Richard Brinsley Sheridan)

This is prettier. The regular way is for a pretty girl to see the pretty flowers; Sheridan's flowery compliment is to imagine the roses as the active figure and the girl as a beautiful flowering ground.

Many a patient, after countless sessions, has quit therapy because he could detect no perceptible improvement in his shrink's condition. (Brendan Francis)

Conventionally the psychoanalyst improves the patient's condition. Francis describes the condition in which the patient criticizes the doctor for failing to improve, for not showing some appreciation of the patient's condition. If the patient improves, should not the doctor?

There are two ways of meeting difficulties: you alter the difficulties, or you alter yourself meeting them. (Phyllis Bottome)

There are similar remarks: **Are you changing your mind, or is your mind changing you?** and **If you do not get what you like, like what you get.**

Happy are the parents that have no children.
Sir Boyle Roche

All three of these remarks are chiasmuses, in which the order of the terms in the first clause is reversed in the second clause. Obviously chiasmuses reverse the figure/ground relationship. A normal or usual relationship is announced or implied, and then the wit reverses the order of the terms and makes the ground the figure, the figure the ground. What was active becomes passive, and vice versa.

He has not acquired a fortune; the fortune has acquired him. (Bion)

The ordinary picture is of a man getting money; man is the active figure and his fortune is the passive ground. Bion points out that the money can be the active force and acquire the man in that it forces him to behave according to his riches.

Some people are always grumbling because roses have thorns. I am thankful that thorns have roses. (Alphonse Kerr)

Kerr's delightfully sentimental aphorism sees the best in things. He is saying that "some people" put the cart before the horse in that they fail to accentuate the positive and eliminate the negative. The rose is the flower at the top of the thorned bush. Kerr looks up to its apotheosis; others, he says, look down from the crown to the pain beneath.

When a dog bites a man that is not news; but when a man bites a dog that is news. (John B. Bogart)

This famous criterion of newsworthiness shows that in order for an item to be newsworthy, it must represent some new insight and the figure/ground relationship must be restated. News is novelty; newsworthy behavior has to be out of the ordinary.

The deer season just opened. A deer hunter in Ventura County brought in his first man yesterday. (Will Rogers)

We expect him to be a man who is a hunter of deer, not a deer who is a hunter of men.

Some painters transform the sun into a yellow spot, others transform a yellow spot into the sun. (Pablo Picasso)

Part of the magic of art is the way in which representation works. Picasso's chiasmus proposes the average art experience of the sun as a yellow spot, and he combats this with his presumed practice of making a yellow spot stand for the sun. Instead of being reductive, his kind of artist is expansive.

Laws

The way the human mind ordinarily works, in apparent contempt of the logicians, is *conclusion first, premises afterwards.* (Joseph Rickaby)

Conclusions drawn from premises is the official logic. There is a hidden point here, that we may be arguing from premises to conclusion, but we cannot identify them until we reach a conclusion.

Say's Law: Supply creates its own demand.

The Law of Supply and Demand says that demand creates supply. Say points out in his law that in modern times some merchandise is in search of customers. The figure becomes supply and the ground demand. The horse demand used to draw the cart supply. Say states that consumer products produce consumerism.

Imbesi's Law of the Conservation of Filth: In order for something to become clean, something else must become dirty.

From an ecological point of view everything is interdependent. We take heart that it is now the mop not the floor, now the water in the sink not the mop. The regression leads us to believe that finally the sewers and the seas are dirtied. In each process the figure becomes the ground.

To be sure of hitting the target, shoot first and, whatever you hit, call it the target. (Ashleigh Brilliant)

Usually the target is the figure, and the ground is the ground.

Brilliant suggests reversing this procedure, letting any part of an undifferentiated ground become the target by chance, letting ground precede figure.

Notice that the nose was formed to wear spectacles: thus we wear spectacles. (Voltaire)

Designers used the nose as a bridge to support and securespectacles; Voltaire pretends to presume the nose was designed to have spectacles put on it. He puts the spectacles before the nose.

Gertrude Stein remarked to the manager in the sitting room of a nineteenth-century hotel that was overfurnished and had a large collection of small lamps, "If you turn on another of those lights, we'll be in complete darkness."

Miss Stein was making the point that with every little light that was turned on, the darkness of the rest of the room was thrown further forward into our perception. It became the figure and the lights the ground, instead of the other way around.

Stacey returned home after his first vacation abroad, and he didn't look too happy.

"Did you enjoy yourself?" asked his neighbor.

"Well, to tell you the truth, I'm so glad to be home I'm not sorry I went."

The holiday is the figure and the home life the ground, for the first few days; soon the home life is seen against the background of the holiday.

"To my regret, I shall have to decline your invitation because of a subsequent engagement." (Oscar Wilde)

The usual state of affairs is that someone offers you an invitation. Either you accept, or you refuse because of a previous engagement. Wilde posits a position whereby one has accepted, but then declines, due to a subsequent engagement. Something better has come up. The first engagement accepted—the figure—becomes the ground, and the subsequent engagement becomes the figure.

During a long stay in Paris, William Morris very nearly cloistered himself in the restaurants of the Eiffel Tower, not only taking all his meals but even doing much of his writing there.

"You're certainly impressed by the Tower," someone once remarked to him.

"Impressed?" said Morris. "I stay here because it's the only place in Paris where I can avoid seeing the damn thing!"

Morris's loathing of the Eiffel Tower is based on his perception of it as a figure towering above the ground of Paris. His solution is perfect: stay in the loathed place as a ground, and perceive the rest of Paris as a figure.

If I am like someone else, who will be like me?
Leo Rosten

John Kemble was performing one of his favorite parts at some country theater and was interrupted from time to time by the squalling of a child in the balcony, until at length, angered by this rival performance, Kemble walked with solemn steps to the front of the stage and, addressing the audience in his most tragic tones, said, "Ladies and gentlemen, unless the play is stopped, the child cannot possibly go on."

We are accustomed to perceiving the play as the thing and the audience as the ground. This child is so demonstrative that this member of the audience becomes the player, and the play becomes the background.

Oscar Wilde arrived at his club one evening after witnessing a first production of a play that was a complete failure.

"Oscar, how did your play go tonight?" said a friend.

"Oh," was the lofty response, "the play was a great success, but the audience was a failure."

Generally, the audience is seen as a passive ground that judges the figure of the play as a success or failure. But Wilde introduces a third figure, the dramatist, who finds the unsuccessful play a success; hence the passive audience, now raised to the status of a figure, is a failure for failing to perceive the brilliance of the play.

The tragedy of old age is not that one is old, but that one is not young.
Oscar Wilde

Time

In rivers, the water that you touch is the last of what has passed and the first of that which comes: so with time present. (Leonardo da Vinci)

Da Vinci considers the present to be in touch with past and future. The present is the figure linked to the ground of past and future. Leonardo points out, with his metaphor of river water, the seamless link between those areas, where we usually see the distinct entities in abstract terms. Figure becomes ground and ground figure.

The now, the here, through which all future plunges to the past. (James Joyce)

The present is the frame through which the figure of the future rushes into the ground of the past.

Times goes, you say? Ah no!

Alas, Time stays, *we* go. (Austin Dobson)

Our perception of time going away from us in the now toward the past is challenged by Dobson. He says that we decay and die, whereas the idea of time stays in human consciousness. We perceive ourselves as the figure past which a field of time proceeds; Dobson sees time as an absolute.

George Bernard Shaw was showing a friend a bust of himself made by Rodin:

"It's a funny thing about that bust," he said. "As times goes on it seems to get younger and younger."

Actually, Shaw was getting older and older. He was pulling away from the bust into decrepitude, and it was his egotism that

> The only wealth which you will keep forever is the wealth
> which you have given away.
> Martial

makes him see the bust this way. It is like being on a stationary railway train in a station when another train is pulling out, and you think that your own train is pulling out in the opposite direction. Figure and ground are completely confused. The view from the train windows is only of the other train; there are few other clues if our train's engine is turning over and making noise. Sometimes it is only when the whole train has passed by that you realize you've been stationary. Another factor is our nervousness and anxiety to depart, even in the wrong direction. Other examples of this phenomenon are when we look at the moon through moving clouds and the moon appears to move, and when high buildings viewed from below against a sky with moving clouds appear to be falling. In a small aircraft, it is difficult to see that the aircraft is performing maneuvers and not the ground.

We are always doing, says he, something for posterity, but I would fain see posterity do something for us. (Joseph Addison)

Since posterity is in the future, when we will be the past, it cannot do anything for us, though we can act with it in mind.

Excuse me, I didn't recognize you. I've changed so much. (Oscar Wilde)

Usually nonrecognition is concluded by "You've changed so much." The spectator is the passive ground against which the active figure is seen to have moved out of recognition. Wilde says that the observer brings his nature and prejudices to the affair. Wilde has changed so much that he does not want to, or even cannot, recognize a person from a past life. Another aspect of this remark is the way it confuses our internal and external nature: instead of commenting on the other person's appearance, Wilde hints at internal change.

In order to play in a play called *Rosemary*, the actor John Drew shaved off his mustache, thereby greatly changing his appearance. Shortly afterward he met Max Beerbohm in the lobby of a London theater but could not just then recall who the latter was. Beerbohm's memory was better.

"Oh, Mr. Drew," he said, "I'm afraid you don't recognize me without your mustache."

Beerbohm's story echoes Wilde's. The change in Drew's external appearance is taken for a change in his internal makeup. His perception of Beerbohm as a figure is presumed to be altered by his background as a clean-shaven man.

Flags flapping aid the wind's turbulence. (Anthony Earnshaw)

Cause and effect are inverted here. The wind is the cause, the flapping flags the effect; Earnshaw makes the flags assistants to the wind's turbulence. After all, stones in river beds cause currents and whirlpools. Earnshaw sees that the relation between things is not simple, but reciprocal: the way to say this is to say the opposite to redress the balance.

It's not the size of the ship; it's the size of the waves. (Little Richard)

Boats are manufactured in varying sizes, appropriate for different cargoes and weather and water conditions. Obviously both the size of the ship and the size of the waves need to be taken into account if the waves come over the boat. Little Richard emphasizes the rarer view, that the size of the waves matters, something over which we have no control, whereas we can control the size of the ship.

An American who had gone to England during the Second World War was wearied by a seemingly interminable season of fog and rain. One day he glanced out of his window at the barrage balloons that through the mist could be seen at their cable ends in the sky and asked, "Why don't they just cut the ropes on those things and let the place sink?"

He knew that the barrage balloons were anchored to England; he pretends that England is a dead weight anchored to the barrage balloons. The balloons' lightness is ambiguous—is it to keep England up or to keep themselves up?

One hand washes the other.
Lenny Moscowitz

> I must be cruel, only to be kind.
> William Shakespeare

Tell me, was it you or your brother who was killed in the war? (Rev. Spooner)

Of the two brothers, one would now be in the ground, and one would be the figure. Spooner does not know which it is. Presumably the man he is talking to does. He cannot be the one killed in the war. But what is his name? Spooner is alternating between figure and ground, between Bill and Ben, whereas his listener is clearly either Bill, background Ben; or Ben, background Bill.

An optimist thinks this is the best of all possible worlds, and a pessimist fears this is so. (Anonymous)

This is the same world, perceived as a figure against different grounds of expectation. The optimist has lower expectations and is more easily pleased. The pessimist makes greater demands. He sees greener, richer fields against which the world looks tawdry.

A cinema attendant was asked what business was like.

"To tell you the truth," he said, "when the place isn't half-full, it's half-empty."

The cinema attendant oscillates between optimism and pessimism. He can see the people in the seats, or he can see the empty seats.

'Twixt the optimist and pessimist
The difference is droll:
The optimist sees the doughnut
But the pessimist sees the hole.
(McLandburgh Wilson)

A schoolmistress was teaching geography in such a fashion that her pupils were bored to tears. But one little boy looked more than just bored. He looked completely blank.

"Tell me," the teacher asked him, "do you have trouble hearing me?"

"No," he replied. "I have trouble listening."

The active and passive roles in perception are distinguished here: hearing is merely a sense perception, whereas listening is comprehension. The teacher's bad teaching is an undifferentiated field to the little boy's passive perception. He cannot pick a figure out of it; there is nothing in it for him to listen to.

Actor Victor Spinetti tells the story of often traveling from London to Cardiff and back again by train. He found the weekly journey exhausting. He had to go there and back very often. Then he found the answer: there was no need for him to go to Cardiff or

---

Doing just the opposite is also a form of imitation.
G. C. Lichtenberg

---

to London; all he had to do was to get on the train—it was going there anyway. He found himself much less tired.

Spinetti's point is that if you sit, it goes; it takes you, willy-nilly. If you try to go, you tire yourself. Be the passive passenger; let the train take the strain. The train is the moving figure, and the passengers are the ground it takes there.

12. Visual
FIGURE/GROUND REVERSAL

This very early bit of art (40), made c. 25,000 B.C., shows how either figure or ground can be read. These pictures were made by placing the hand against the wall of the cave and filling a bone blowpipe with pigment, then blowing color all around the hand. When the hand is removed, you're left with a picture of where it has been. Hands can be colored and applied to the wall, or they can be applied to the wall and the wall colored.

A modern joke about the same subject (41) has a silly person painting the road black around the center line markings, rather than painting the markings on the road. There is an extra absurdity here in that such roads are already black tarmac and do not need to be painted—although cartoon roads do.

40. Hands (Prehistoric)

41. Drawing
(esspé [Pierre Stora])

The story is told of the Upside-Down Room, where all the furnishings, drapes, pictures and fireplace are upside down. The rugs and furniture are fastened to the ceiling, while the floor contains a single object—an elaborate chandelier thrust upward from the center. A guest at a party in the house has too much to drink and passes out. He is carried into the Upside-Down Room and placed on the "ceiling" (really the floor) midway between the wall and the chandelier. When he awakens he has a bad time of it.

In *The Haunted Swing* (42), the swing and the people in it were virtually stationary, while the room was swung around them.

The author entered a "Crazy Room" at Blackpool, England. It was a well-lit sitting room containing bookcases, occasional tables with lamps, a TV set, and so on. Coming in through the short wall, traversing the room, and going out through the opposite wall was a metal pole with two long benches attached to it. Members of the public were inadequately strapped onto these benches. The attendant left the room, locking the door behind him. Nervous glances at the ceiling, scuffed by shoes. Are we going to be whirled around in this room? Slowly we are all turned on our benches until we are upside-down in the room and gradually revolved at a walking pace to an upright position in the room, and so on for several revolutions.

We realize that the room is being turned around us, but the illusion is so strong that it seems unbelievable. Sensations of nausea attend our motion. Even if you shut your eyes, the sound of the turning makes you think you are still moving. The attendant stops the movement when the room is in an upright position. Relief. Then he turns the room in the other direction, and there is a fearful sensation of falling backward as you slowly tumble heels over head in this fake sitting room in the presence of strangers, at night near the beach in summer.

In Bianca Juarez's *Apple Tree* (43) the stalk of an apple becomes the trunk of a tree. But trees do grow from apples; when the apple falls on the ground it grows into a tree, which itself grows apples, in the relentless pattern of natural growth and decay, growth and decay.

42. The Haunted Swing
(Nineteenth Century)

43. Apple Tree
(Bianca Juarez)

In the Pisa cartoon by esspé (44) we find a reversal of what we already know of the relation between the figure of the Tower of Pisa and the ground of Pisa. The plumb bob suggests that maybe the Tower is perpendicular and the landscape tilted.

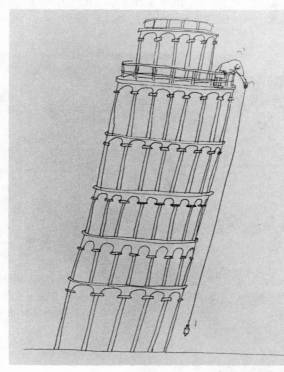

44. Drawing
(esspé [Pierre Stora])

Ian Walker's "slipshots" (45–48) follow similar reasoning. He finds things in the urban landscape that are not vertical, photographs them, and then prints rectangular photographs with the thing vertical and the rest of the world on the tilt. The bollard and the "bump" sign have both been adjusted by collisions with vehicles. The statue is thrusting into the wind, and the silhouette of a pedestrian has moved in its mounting. The ground is made to follow these figures. Walker comments: "This is one of the fundamental elements of photography—the rigorous way in which the framing of a picture controls our reading of its content."

45. Cardiff, 1980
(Ian Walker)

46

47

46. New York, 1980
(Ian Walker)

47. London, 1980
(Ian Walker)

48. Cardiff, 1981
(Ian Walker)

48

13. Verbal
SELF-REFERENCE

Verb Agrees with Noun

In tautology, similar terms are linked by a verb that does not imply action. Of the two forms of self-reference considered here, the first is the one in which an active verb refers to its own noun.

When there was a water shortage, the silly party proposed to dilute the water to make it go further.

To dilute the water is to water the water. We dilute many things, the silly party argues, so why not water? But water is the one thing one cannot dilute.

I wish he would explain his explanation. (Lord Byron)

> The unnatural, that too is natural.
> Goethe

If his explanation is not adequate, not comprehensible, what makes Byron think that an explaining of his explanation would be any better? The explainings of the explanations would regress infinitely.

No explanation ever explains the necessity of making one. (Elbert Hubbard)

Hubbard questions the very nature of explanations, which pose the same facts in a different light. How does one explain the need for explanations? Surely the facts should speak for themselves?

Thank you for giving me the pleasure of giving pleasure to you. (Ashleigh Brilliant)

To give pleasure is itself a pleasure. Perhaps giving pleasure is more of a pleasure than receiving pleasure. (Compare with "You only have what you have given away.")

Love is an irresistible desire to be irresistibly desired. (Robert Frost)

The mutual force of love for each partner is to be loved. Each wants the other to love him.

I consider you unfortunate because you have never been unfortunate. (Seneca)

Seneca thinks of the person who has had an uneventful, successful life as unfortunate because such a person has not had the opportunity to learn fortitude.

> My life has a superb cast—but I can't figure out the plot.
> Ashleigh Brilliant

Nothing succeeds like success. (Alexandre Dumas)

There is a snowball factor in success, a way in which the successful person is asked to do more things than the not-so-successful person. In this sense, success is self-verifying and self-supporting.

In the next three examples, the verb is in agreement with a clause that contains the same verb.

A man can do what he wants, but not want what he wants. (Arthur Schopenhauer)

To want what you want is a redundancy. (Compare with Henry Blossom's tautology, "I want what I want when I want it.") Either you want it or you do not. (Compare also with Tolstoy's "Boredom—the desire for desires.")

BRAIN. An apparatus with which we think that we think. (Ambrose Bierce)

Thinking about thinking is an act of self-reference often indulged in. (W. H. Auden quoted the anonymous, "When we think a thing, the thing we think is not the thing we think we think, but only the thing we think we think we think.")

It is often easier to hide something than to hide the fact that you are hiding something. (G. C. Lichtenberg)

To physically conceal a thing is one thing, but to hide the fact—

face to face—that you have hidden something from someone posits the possibility of revealing by one's appearance the fact of one's subterfuge.

Its Own Self

A writer can be his own typist or editor. A farmer can be his own mechanic or accountant. However, some ideas, when referring to the person's own self, are especially revealing.

Every man is his own chief enemy. (Anarcharsis)

An enemy is the opposite of oneself, a person whom one dislikes and fights, someone who does one wrong. To be one's own enemy is to dislike and fight yourself. Does the person who is his own worst enemy know it? If he knows he is, he can act on it; if he does not, his actions will be less than effective.

I am my own ancestor. (Iphicrates)

People boast of their ancestors as if this had a bearing on their own worth. Iphicrates says he is his own ancestor, that a judgment of his worth must be made solely on the basis of him. He has given himself the attributes he has.

He is a self-made man and worships his creator. (John Bright, on Disraeli)

The syllogism here is: He is a self-made man. He worships his creator. Therefore, he worships himself.

To worship, to adore as of a god, is not something you do to yourself. You are meant to have a more critical view of someone you know so well. The creator is God. Does this man think of himself as a god, Bright asks.

It is easy to look down on others; to look down on ourselves is the difficulty. (Charles Mordaunt Peterborough)

The physical act of looking down, as from a balcony, is used here metaphorically to mean "judge as lacking." Peterborough's wit is to invite us to look down on ourselves—a physical impossibility, but occasionally a moral necessity.

If you ever find happiness by hunting for it, you will find it, as the old woman did her lost spectacles, safe on her own nose all the time. (Josh Billings)

Happiness, the popular philosopher Billings tells us, is to be found at home, in ourselves, not out in the physical world of pleasures and diversions. We will find it in the way we look at things, right under our noses, and it will be barely discernible.

An intellectual is someone whose mind watches itself. (Albert Camus)

For the mind to watch the mind rather than the rest of the world, it would have to think of itself as a thing. An intellectual is someone so mindful of his mind that he watches it at work.

A sergeant of the criminal court told a prisoner, "If ever there was a clearer case of a man robbing his master, that case was this case."

You can observe a lot just by watchin'.
Yogi Berra

This case is clearer than itself. It is such a clear case of a man robbing his master that it is a paradigm case, and all cases, including this one, must take it as an example.

The most beautiful thing in the world is, of course, the world itself. (Wallace Stevens)

As we read this, we have a moment to think of what we might nominate as the most beautiful thing in the world before the poet pulls the rug from under us and nominates the world, which both contains everything and is a wonderful mechanism in itself.

14. Visual
SELF-REFERENCE

Doing and Done

We find our two types of verbal self-reference—where the verb agrees with the noun and where a thing is related to its own self—in visual self-reference. In Raymond Savignac's *Astral Peinture Émail* (49) a painter paints a painting that in turn is painting the picture of the painter. For a painting just to paint would not be enough; to make this point there has to be some circularity.

In Les Coleman's *Lolly/tongue* (50), the licked is the licker; the lolly is at the same time a tongue by metamorphosis. There is an identity between a lolly and a tongue: the one is made to fit on the other.

49. Astral Peinture Émail
(Raymond Savignac)

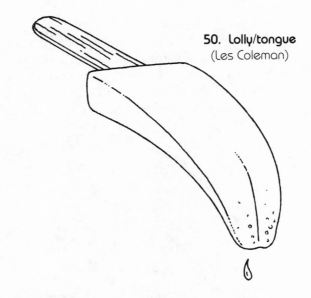

50. Lolly/tongue
(Les Coleman)

Its Own Self

Tony Blundell's *Brokedown Lorry* (51) pulls itself uphill. It rescues itself. It refers to itself rather than to another vehicle.

51. Brokedown Lorry
(Tony Blundell)

Masters dangle carrots in front of donkeys' noses to encourage them to greater efforts. Anthony Earnshaw's *Unicorn with a Carrot* (52) hangs a carrot from its own horn and tempts itself to go on to various exertions. Does the unicorn ever get the carrot? We provide our own incentives, and when we have achieved them, we set new ones. Or has someone else hung a carrot there?

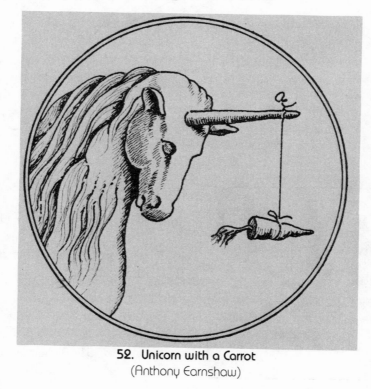

52. Unicorn with a Carrot
(Anthony Earnshaw)

Les Coleman's *Cut Along the Dotted Line* (53) is a drawing of scissors cutting out scissors. The scissors that are being cut out are quite a useless pair of unmoving, limp paper scissors, but they are scissors

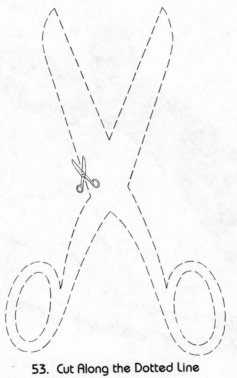

53. Cut Along the Dotted Line
(Les Coleman)

The author's *Fear Itself* (54) is of a man pursued by his own shadow. The shadow is no longer passive but active, and the man is running from himself. It is a solid and predatory shadow that does not just tag along, but is the active force in the relationship.

54. Fear Itself
(Patrick Hughes)

15. Verbal
SELF-CONTRADICTION

This area of wit is adjacent to the contradiction in terms and self-reference. In self-reference, the idea merely refers to itself. In the contradiction in terms, contradictory concepts from opposite ends of a continuum of meaning are linked. In self-contradiction, an idea refers to itself and contradicts itself. One major form in self-contradiction is when the linked terms are the same term but in positive and negative form.

To be ignorant of one's ignorance is the malady of the ignorant. (A. B. Alcott)

This ignorance of one's ignorance is self-referential and contradictory. The ignorant think that they know something. This differs from a contradiction in terms in that the opposing terms are not ignorance and knowledge but ignorance and ignorance.

In these matters the only certainty is that there is nothing certain. (Pliny the Elder)

"The only certainty" is pitted against "nothing certain." There is a paradoxical aspect to this remark: if there is nothing certain, then even "the only certainty" is not certain, and so the remark chases its own tail.

At least I have the modesty to admit that lack of modesty is one of my failings. (Hector Berlioz)

Berlioz's self-knowledge is self-contradictory: is he modest or not? He modestly admits to a lack of modesty, but is this immodest? Richard Burton wrote, **They are proud in humility, proud in that they are not proud.** Wyndham Lewis said, **The English certainly and fiercely pride themselves on never praising themselves.**

Self-contradiction can come from a full self-awareness:

I have made mistakes, but I have never made the mistake of claiming that I never made one. (James Gordon Bennett)

Bennett's aphorism recognizes that the mistake of invulnerability is the greatest mistake.

Hegel was right when he said that we learn from history that men can never learn anything from history. (George Bernard Shaw)

When we read history we see that mistakes are repeated, espe-

---

Trapped, like a trap in a trap.
Dorothy Parker

> I am not sincere, not even when I say I am not.
> Jules Renard

cially from a Hegelian point of view. We see that events do not develop, but that history repeats itself.

Notice that in this form of bull there is usually a negative—a never or a not—to set the same terms at odds with each other.

My advice is that you should never take my advice. (Ashleigh Brilliant)

The noun "advice" here is linked with the verb "to take advice" by the negative "never." Ogden Nash's **If you don't want to work you have to work to earn enough money so that you won't have to work** has two negatives—"don't want to work" and "won't have to work"—linked by a positive, "you have to work."

As a philosophically minded biologist once observed, "If the human brain were so simple that we could understand it, we would be so simple that we could not." (W. A. Clouston)

To study a thing using itself as the tool is a problem of self-reference.

Sometimes in self-contradictory bulls the two terms that are in opposition are loosely linked:

You've no idea what a poor opinion I have of myself—and how little I deserve it. (W. S. Gilbert)

Gilbert's "I have a poor opinion of myself" and "how little I deserve it" are linked by a mere dash. "To have" and "to deserve" are verbs that can describe different things; lots of us think that what we have and what we deserve are very different things.

Artemus Ward's **Let us be happy and live within our means, even if we have to borrow the money to do it with** is almost a straightforward contradiction in terms. "Let us live within our means" and "we have to borrow the money" are opposite ends of the spectrum of solvency, but there is a huge element of self-reference in borrowing money to live within one's means.

If I've done anything I'm sorry for, I'm willing to be forgiven. (Edward N. Westcott)

"To be sorry" and "to be forgiven" are active and passive verbs standing at opposite ends of the continuum of blame.

I have always thought that all women should marry and that all men should remain bachelors. (Benjamin Disraeli)

"All women should marry" and "all men should remain bachelors" stand at opposite ends of the married/unmarried axis, but who is going to marry whom? They are linked by Disraeli's "I have always thought that" and "[I have always thought] that."

Towns should be built in the country. The air there is purer. (Henry Mounier)

The "mistake," made here by Mounier's character Monsieur Prudhomme, is in the double bill of "Towns should be built in the country" and "The air [in the country] is purer [than town air]."

Building towns in the country will make the country into the town, and the pure country air into impure town air. This is self-defeating.

Self-exemplification

This is an aspect of self-contradiction where the proposition disobeys its own injunction. William Safire's readers in *The New York Times* provided him with a large number of grammatical rules of this order:

> **Do not put statements in the negative form.**
> **And don't start a sentence with a conjunction.**
> **It is incumbent on one to avoid archaisms.**
> **If you reread your work, you will find on rereading that a great deal of repetition can be avoided by rereading and editing.**
> **Never use a long word when a diminutive one will do.**
> **Unqualified superlatives are the worst of all.**
> **De-accession euphemisms.**
> **If any word is improper at the end of a sentence, a linking verb is.**
> **Avoid trendy locutions that sound flaky.**
> **Never, ever use repetitive redundancies.**
> **Also, avoid awkward or affected alliteration.**

A tired exclamation mark is a question mark.

Stanislaw Lec

Last, but not least, avoid clichés like the plague; seek viable alternatives.

Each of these instructions exemplifies the fault that it castigates.

Nigel Rees, a collector of graffiti, cites a graffito from Pompeii: **Everyone writes on the walls but me.**

It may well have been that up until the moment of writing "me," he did not write on the walls like everyone else; but having written his remark, he contradicts himself. Compare the contemporary photograph (55) by Roger Perry.

55. Words Do Not Mean Anything Today
(Roger Perry)

> All gods *were* immortal.
> Stanislaw Lec

Nigel Rees reports three contemporary graffiti that belong to this genre:

Hypochondria is the one disease I have not got.

Procrastinate now!

I've told you for the fifty-thousandth time, stop exaggerating.

An exchange that exemplifies self-contradiction:

Young man: "Why do philosophers ask so many questions?"

Old philosopher: "Why shouldn't philosophers ask so many questions?"

Against Itself

Just as in straight self-reference, where one thing refers to itself, in self-contradiction there is an area where a thing or person contradicts itself or himself.

I can never be satisfied with anyone who would be blockhead enough to have me. (Abraham Lincoln, in a letter to Mrs. O. H. Browning)

Lincoln's self-negating proposal, composed of distaste for himself and for anyone who would have him, is perhaps the origin of Groucho Marx's remark that "I would refuse to join any club that would have me as a member."

On a stone placed at a ford in a river is the inscription: "When this stone is covered it is dangerous to ford here."

The difficulty with this sign is that the inscription is placed on the stone itself. If it was placed on a nearby wall, drawing attention to the particular stone whose height announced the fordability of the river, there would be no self-contradiction and fewer people drowned.

A drunkard was fined by a judge for being drunk and could not pay the fine. The judge remarked, "If you hadn't got drunk with your money, you'd be able to pay the fine."

If he had not got drunk with his money, there would be no fine, the drunkard could well reply. The case itself is about his drunkenness.

According to John Gunther, an American journalist in Japan wrote to a friend and added the note, "Don't know if this will ever arrive because the Japanese censor may open it." A few days afterward he received a note from the Japanese post office saying, "The statement in your letter is not correct. We do not open letters."

"And have you made your will, madam?"

"Indeed I have. All of my fortune goes to the doctor that saves my life."

If she does defeat death by the efforts of the doctor nominated as heir, he will not inherit because she will not be dead.

Contradictory self-reference is found in **Hofstadter's Law: It always takes longer than you expect, even when you take into account Hofstadter's Law.** (Douglas Hofstadter) and in:

Boquist's Exception: If for every rule there is an exception, then we have established that there is an exception to every rule. If we accept "For every rule there is an exception" as a rule, then we must concede that there may not be an exception after all, since the rule states that there is always the possibility of exception, and if we follow it to its logical end we must agree that there can be an exception to the rule that for every rule there is an exception. (Bill Boquist)

> I am writing to tell you I have nothing to say.
> Ashleigh Brilliant

16. Visual
SELF-CONTRADICTION

Glen Baxter's *Man Sawing* (56) illustrates the story of the man who sawed off the branch he was kneeling on, a relative of the man who painted himself into the corner of the room. The man is cutting the rug from under himself.

Just as in verbal self-contradiction the linked terms are in positive and negative form, in the drawing of a girl knitting by Claude Serre (57) the positive knitting she practices at the top of her dress is linked by the wool to the negative unraveling taking place at her hem.

In his *Crime and Reward* (58) Marcel Mariën has noticed that axes—which chop down trees—are made of trees, that trees attack trees. This is a self-contradiction. To bring out the ax's treachery he sticks twigs into its wooden handle to show it as a growing thing.

56. Man Sawing
(Glen Baxter)

57. Drawing
(Claude Serre)

58. Crime and Reward
(Marcel Mariën)

In *The Viper* (59), by the same artist, the tree harbors a viper in its bosom. The ax head is fixed to a branch of the tree, ready to begin its bloody work from within the enemy camp. Mariën's strategy in these complementary pieces is to add twigs to an ax, and add an ax to twigs, to point up the self-contradictory relations between timber and trees.

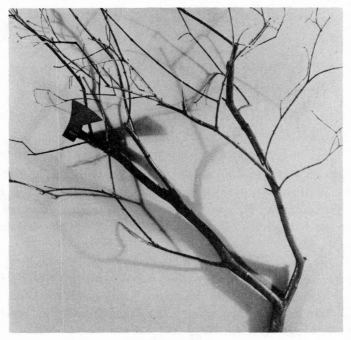

59. The Viper
(Marcel Mariën)

17. Verbal
MIND AND MATTER

A rich source of bulls is the dualism between conception and perception, idea and reality, art and life. This area is like the figure/ground reversal in that a reversal is operative, only here instead of the ground being put before the figure an idea deduced from life is imposed on life.

Extract from a Malay newspaper:

An oppressive heat wave passed over Calcutta yesterday. In the city the temperature rose to the record figure of about 108 degrees. This sudden rise of temperature was responsible for the intolerable heat.

In fact the heat was measured in terms of temperature, rather than that the rise in temperature gave the Indians the heat. (This remark is akin to Calvin Coolidge's tautology, "When large numbers of men are out of work unemployment results.") However, I have placed it at the beginning of this section because of the active force our conception of heat—measured in degrees Fahrenheit—has on our perception of the intolerable heat.

Notice in a newspaper:

Because of lack of space a number of births have been held over until next week.

The births have not been held over, the announcements have. These conceptions exist as facts apart from their mention in the paper. Some of the comedy of this line lies in the contrast between the reality of birth and its smudged representation in a small weekly newspaper.

A man looked up from his newspaper and said to his wife, "I'll never understand how it is that people always die in alphabetical order."

The way in which people's deaths are formally listed in a paper, arranged from the various reports of the different deaths, is here taken as fact rather than as a listing that enables people to look up the details with which they are concerned. Some order is imposed on the shapeless fact of death, but the man is wrong to think that death follows neat rules.

A man wrote to the *Guinness Book of Records* and claimed that he should be included. He explained that at one time he had been the youngest person in the world.

This is true of all of us. The youngest person in the world is a role for which the actors change very rapidly, many times a second. The part of oldest person in the world does not change nearly so rapidly; we all start the race, but some of us drop out far from the finishing line, which is currently being gradually extended.

A man who was four feet six inches tall offered his services to a circus. He claimed he was the tallest dwarf in the world.

The smallest dwarf in the world is an idea that fits well with reality: there is one. But as dwarfishness rises toward normal height, the concept becomes blurred and reality intervenes. Who is to draw the line, and how can our candidate assure us on what side of the line he stands?

He pulled up his car beside the oldest inhabitant of the village.
"And you're ninety-seven years of age?" he asked.
"Indeed I am."
"Have you lived in the village all your life?"
"Oh, no. Not yet."

These ideas of the oldest, youngest, shortest, and so on are readily contrasted with reality. The questioner really means "all

---

Bachelors' wives and old maids' children are always perfect.
Nicolas Chamfort

---

your life up till now," but the answerer answers to "all your life up to death." There is a hidden meaning—"Are you to die in the village?" The old person seems content to regard his death.

A visitor to a small village accosted an elderly local and asked who was the oldest inhabitant.

"We haven't got one now, sir," was the reply; "we had one, but he died three weeks ago."

These jokes depend on keeping something fixed that is really a relation—on holding on to the idea while ignoring moving reality. If the person who was the oldest inhabitant died, that position has not died with him; there would immediately be a new, younger, oldest inhabitant.

Consider also:

Incomprehensibly, the last coach of the train on a normal route kept getting smashed up by vandals. A porter came up with an idea. "Leave the last coach off!"

The idea "the last coach" is taken as a thing rather than part of a series, a relation in reality. Once you take off the last coach, the next-to-last coach becomes the last coach, and so on.

A cockney said, "I believe the end of this 'ere rope is cut off."

If the end is cut off, another end appears. A rope will always have two ends; that is what we call the point at which rope becomes absence of rope.

> Railway lines do meet—in your eye.
> Foster-Harris

"Hey, John, what's your earliest memory?"

"Er . . . I don't remember!"

The earliest memory, the one that he cannot remember, is presumably before his earliest memory, one that he can remember. By definition an earliest memory must be remembered.

Overheard in a hotel:

"It's eight o'clock, sir!"

"Why the devil didn't you tell me that before?"

The guest really means "Why the devil didn't you wake me before?" He did not want to be told it was eight o'clock at six o'clock. The idea of being awakened in time is here pitted against the reality of a particular time of day.

"Hey, Bill, will you hurry up? Haven't you an appointment with Paul?"

"I have, but I told him I'd be late so I've lots of time yet."

Often people arrive later than the appointed time. This man is going to arrive on time late. The precise time of meeting is contrasted with the idea of being late.

"Hey, Arthur, what was the score of this afternoon's game?"

"Three to one."

"Who won?"

"Three."

Three will always win over one. Three is not the name of the team, it is their achievement on that day. Three is the name we give to the reality of their total effort; it is how we describe one terrific shot, one lucky fumble, and one own goal; whereas Crewe Alexandra Football Club is the name for the eleven players who represent the board of directors and the supporters.

> Where there is a great deal of light, the shadows are deeper.
> Goethe

Have you heard about the plain girl who came in second in a beauty contest?

She was the only entrant.

When you first hear of the girl coming in second you think, well, she did not win, but she did come in second. When you then hear there was only one entrant you realize how plain she must have been. She was so plain she was plainer than herself. Or she achieved a degree of plainness as yet unachieved, second out of one.

The American had been fishing for two weeks at Ballinahinch without getting a bite. On the last day of his vacation he caught a small salmon.

"Burroughs," he said to his fishing guide as the fish was landed, "that salmon cost me five hundred dollars."

"Well now, sir," comforted Burroughs, "aren't you the lucky man you didn't catch two."

The fishing guide figures if one cost five hundred dollars, two would cost one thousand dollars. The realistic arithmetic is that if one cost five hundred dollars, two will cost two hundred and fifty dollars each, since five hundred dollars is the price of the trip. The gillie multiplies where he should divide. He brings the idea of the price of fish from the fish shop, instead of attending to the reality of the price of the American's trip.

> The telescope makes the world smaller,
> the microscope makes the world larger.
>
> G. K. Chesterton

The two tinkers had been walking all day along the Connemara roads. Wearily they came to a signpost. One examined it.

"How far is it to Clifden?"

"Only ten miles."

"That's good. It will only be five miles each."

If you divide ten by two you do get five. You could divide ten eggs between two people, and each would get five. That is the idea. The reality of walking is different. If each tinker walks five miles they will between them have traversed ten miles, but the same five miles—only taking them halfway to Clifden.

The farmer's wife told Sarah, the family servant, that five shillings would be deducted from her wages if the family had to cook their breakfast themselves. A few mornings later Sarah staggered down long after the day had started.

"Sarah, we had to get our own breakfast again."

"Well, aren't I paying you for it?"

The employers become the servants of the servant who has become the employer. The servant thinks of herself as being paid in full, then spending part to pay the farmer's family to get breakfast when she comes down late. This is in contrast to the reality, which is that she is a servant who is being docked pay for her bad timekeeping.

An extremely unattractive man claimed that he had been very beautiful as a baby, but that he had been exchanged by the gypsies.

If "he" had been exchanged by the gypsies, he would no longer be he but another. His ugliness would travel with him. This gag works because it does not use names. Call him "John," and call his substitute "James." If attractive John is now with the gypsies, and unattractive James is talking of his past beauty, we should understand that the beauty travels with the person. He cannot remain with his identity and beauty changed.

Mark Twain used to tell a pathetic story of his childhood. It seems, according to the story, that Twain was born twins. He and his twin looked so much alike that no one, not even their mother, could tell them apart. One day, while the nurse was bathing them, one of them slipped in the bathtub and was drowned. No one ever knew which twin it was that drowned.

"And therein," says Mark Twain, "was the tragedy. Everyone thought I was the one that lived, but I wasn't. It was my brother who lived. I was the one that was drowned."

So I am my brother, and I am dead. Twain asks whether "I" is the sum of those experiences from childhood to now, or whether it is a name? This is the difference between the idea of a person and

the person. It was the idea of a person that died and a real person—
whoever it is—that lived.

**The Argonauts were ordered by the gods to complete their long
journey in one and the same ship—the *Argo*—against the certainty
of the boat's gradual deterioration. Over the course of the voyage
the Argonauts slowly replaced each piece of the ship, "so that they
ended with an entirely new ship, without having to alter either its
name or its form."** (Homer)

The name of a thing, as opposed to the reality of a thing, is
discussed here. The ship is still the *Argo*, although it is made of
quite different materials. By the same process, we human beings
are quite different people from what we were a few months ago; we
are made of different materials though we are still in the same
form. In this story, the idea or form or name takes precedence over
the mundane reality of the materials. There is a similar story told
of **Washington's "original" ax, owned by a collector, that had three
new heads and two new handles since the first President's time.** (It

is also told of the ax that cut off Mary, Queen of Scots' head.) We might ask, is it the ax with which he chopped down the tree or not? It is true that none of the original materials remain. As the ax remained in use and needed replacement of parts, so it is still the same ax conceptually, if not in actuality.

Mark Twain often received photographs from men whose friends had made the men believe that they looked like him. Discovering that his home was beginning to run over with pictures of these aspirants to fame, Twain determined to relieve himself of the burden of answering the heavy correspondence, and so had his printer strike off a few hundred copies of the following form letter:

"My dear Sir: I thank you very much for your letter and your photograph. In my opinion you are more like me than any other of my numerous doubles. I may even say that you resemble me more closely than I do myself. In fact, I intend to use your picture to shave by. Yours thankfully, S. Clemens."

Twain's final gag, that he intends to use the resembling photos to shave by, puts the idea of the resemblance to the test of reality. If they are so like, are they lifelike enough to grow hair to be shaved?

Mrs. Williams brought her dear departed husband's photograph to the shop.

"Could you enlarge this?"

"Certainly, madam."

> Work is the refuge of people who have nothing better to do.
> Oscar Wilde

"And could you remove his hat?"

"We could touch it up for you—but on which side was his hair parted?"

"Are you daft? Surely you will see that when you take off his hat!"

One can take from the photograph only what it has taken from reality. When the hat is taken off it is not hair that is revealed, but the photographic paper. A photo stands in relation to reality, but not in a one-to-one relation.

Cordell Hull is an extremely cautious speaker, striving always for scientific accuracy. One day on a train, a friend pointed to a fine flock of sheep grazing in a field.

"Look, those sheep have just been sheared," he said.

Hull studied the flock. "Sheared on this side, anyway," he admitted.

This splendid skepticism is along the same lines as the hair in the photograph. Hull only trusts his eyes, the photograph only represents what is passed through the eye of the camera. Hull does not attend to the bizarre idea that someone might shear the sheep on the railway side only and that the sheep would all remain in that position: he just tells reality as he can see it.

Lost between decks on the great Atlantic liner only an hour after putting to sea, McCormick had to look for help to find his cabin.

"What was the number?" asked the steward.

"I couldn't tell you," said McCormick, "but I'd know it because it had a lighthouse outside the porthole."

The changing nature of reality is debated in this joke. McCormick sees his cabin as complete with a view of a lighthouse; the steward sees it as having a varying view through the porthole. It is the same cabin but with a different view. (Compare this story with the story of the unmoving railway lines in the section on the verbal obvious).

A glazier repaired fifty windows before he realized he had a crack in his glasses.

This man imposes his perception of the world on reality. (In Edgar Allan Poe's story *The Sphinx*, there is a bug clinging to a window that is perceived as a monster on a distant hill.) A misconception takes the place of a perception.

Have you heard about the explorer who paid ten pounds for a sheet of sandpaper? He thought it was a map of the Sahara Desert.

The relation between a sheet of sandpaper and the Sahara Desert is one of conceptualized diminution, just as a map is; but a sheet of sandpaper is not a map of the Sahara Desert. We have a vague idea of the desert as of undifferentiated sand, but that does not sit well with the harsh reality of its many features. Such a map would be useless.

And there was the householder who rushed the decoration of his home so that he'd have it finished before the pot of paint ran out.

> The same water that drives the mill, decayeth it.
> Stephen Gosson

The idea of rushing the painting will not affect the reality of the amount of paint in the pot. There is a similar gag in a joke letter:

I am writing this letter slowly, as I know you do not read quickly.

The relationship between the speed of production and the speed of perception is not one-to-one.

George Bernard Shaw was asked for his views on youth.
"I think," he said, "that it is wasted on the young."

Youth is an idea, and the young are the reality. Youth is freshness, vitality, creative juice; the young are callow, spotty youths. Shaw would like that stuff "youth" for mature people like himself, who would know how to use it.

Alcohol, taken in sufficient quantities, produces all the effects of intoxication. (Oscar Wilde)

Wilde has two sorts of intoxication in mind: the genuine excitement given, perhaps, by poetry, or love, or life; and the ersatz weakness and light-headedness given by drink. The first intoxication is an idea of perfect excitement; the second, the reality of drunkenness.

The best cure for insomnia is to get a lot of sleep. (W. C. Fields)

Fields's silly statement makes fun of the formal medical definition of sleeplessness by contrasting it with the reality of getting a lot of sleep.

There is only one difference between a madman and me. I am not mad. (Salvador Dali)

To the general public it has seemed that Dali has behaved like a madman. Dali has been the *idea* of a mad person. But the reality is that he is a surrealist artist who has consciously acted in a bizarre and extravagant way rather than being at the mercy, like a mad person, of an *idée fixe*.

ACCIDENT: An inevitable occurrence due to the action of immutable natural laws. (Ambrose Bierce)

Bierce points out that when you drop a cup the forces of friction, gravity, motion, and so on cause the cup to fall and break. Our idea of it is that it is an accident; the reality is that it is inevitable. Oscar Wilde remarked that **Niagara Falls would be more remarkable if the water didn't fall.**

A penny is something we see every day but never look at.
Stephen Potter

---

18. Visual
MIND AND MATTER

In the parallel verbal section of mind and matter, the dualism that the jokester plays on is the attempt to impose a plan on the world. In the comparable visual area, the relation played upon is usually that between art and life. In Grandville's drawing (60), there is a delightful detail (61) where the painting of waves is so realistic that they escape their frame and wet the young lady's cloak. Two-dimensional illusion becomes three-dimensional reality.

Pliny, in his *Natural History*, tells of the artist Zeuxis and his rival Parrhasius. In a duel of illusionism, Zeuxis drew aside the curtain covering his work to reveal a painting of grapes so realistic that some birds flew down and tried to peck them. But he had to admit defeat when, demanding that the drapery covering his rival's picture be drawn aside, he was disappointed to find the curtain itself was painted.

60. An Exhibition Room
(Grandville)

61. An Exhibition Room (detail)
Grandville

Maurice Henry's drawing (62) shows a Greek sculptor at work on the Venus de Milo. The sculpture lost its arms during its long life. Henry argues backward from this position—that if the statue is armless so must the model have been. Part of the joke is about our modern love of the classical period, represented as it is by fragments. Our regard of it is ossified: we do not try to imagine the Venus with arms; we'd rather think that armless is how it was meant to be. Wilde said, "Life imitates art far more than art imitates life."

62. Drawing
(Maurice Henry)

Charles Addams's drawing (63) shows a motorist approaching a sign by the roadside that warns that children cross the road here. The sign is a stylized silhouette of two children with their books. It is designed to be easily readable; it is deduced from the very varied facts of lots of children crossing lots of roads. Addams argues from this conception (drawn from reality) back to reality and imagines a couple of kids just like the ones in the sign, silhouetted and simplified, crossing the road. The driver is surprised that real life is so like the idea of it.

63. Drawing
(Charles Addams)

In the next drawing (64), two married couples are playing cards: two kings and two queens. They are drawn from the drawings on the playing cards. A comparison is being made between the ordinary couples who play cards together and the cards they play with, very distantly drawn from people. The kings and queens on playing cards are very stylized; here they are drawn back into life.

64. Drawing
("H")

Jean Gourmelin's drawing (65) illustrates the paradox of realism. If the theater is to hold a mirror up to nature, then ideally the spectator should be faced with a representation of himself, at the theater, doing what he is doing now. And then who is to say who is the actor and who the real person? The concept and the percept are one.

65. Drawing
J. Gourmelin

Maurice Henry's drawing (66) shows the musician batting a note over a net with his violin. Musical notes are the visual representation of aural fact. They describe the pitch and the duration of the note; they are not things like tennis balls. The contrast here is between musical notation and a physical game. The musician is knocking a concept across a court. Henry is saying that you cannot get hold of an idea.

66. Drawing
(Maurice Henry)

Adelbert Ames's room (67) is made in perspective. That is to say, it is one of a myriad of shapes that from a given point of view will look like an ordinary room. Ames then twice places within his eccentric room two men. In one picture the man with the bow tie is seen as a giant, in the other as a midget. In reality he is simply near or far away. But we perceive him in the context of a regular room. It does not occur to us to see the man in his true size and the room as eccentric.

67. Room
(Adelbert A. Ames)

19. Verbal
NOTHING

"Nothing" contains a number of bulls. The article on negation in the *Encyclopedia of Philosophy* begins, "Nobody knows much about negation. He would of course."

Nobody goes to that restaurant anymore. It's too crowded.

By this is meant "nobody who is anybody." There are two sets of nobodies—those that go, and those that do not.

In the funeral procession of Junia, the sister of Brutus and wife of Cassius, although the images of twenty of the greatest families were borne before her bier, "those of Brutus and Cassius were not displayed; but for that very reason they shone with preeminent luster." (Tacitus)

These two were conspicuous by their absence. Not being there can be as powerful as being there. The perception that someone is not there leads to the conception that that is a powerful statement.

I had rather men should ask why no statue has been erected in my honor, than why one has. (Cato Marcus Porcius)

We all see the statues of worthies that have been erected. To notice that one has not been erected is a more active act: to count them and wonder where it is, or why it has not been constructed.

The old lighthouse keeper had been at his post continuously for thirty years. During that entire period he had been accustomed to a horn going off, practically under his nose, every six minutes, day and night. This was the method for warning the ships. Naturally he grew hardened to this enormous noise and paid no attention to it. Then, one night in his thirty-first year at this post, the horn failed to sound. The old man awoke from a deep sleep.

"What was that?" he cried in alarm.

To be awakened by a silence is oxymoronic. This absence of sound is noted more, because of its rarity, than the ever-present horn going off. Training the mind, as in Pavlov's experiments with dogs, is often a matter of associations withdrawn. The perception of the absence of sound is perceived against a background of noise; usually a noise is perceived against silence.

If people don't want to come, no one's stopping them.
Sol Hurok

---

g composer had written two pieces of music and asked
near them both and say which he preferred. He duly
piece, whereupon Rossini intervened.

ed not play any more," he said, "I prefer the other

did not prefer the other one as a piece of music, but
d not been played. The first was worse than silence.

came back to Dublin I was court-martialed in my
absence and sentenced to death in my absence, so I said they could
shoot me in my absence. (Brendan Behan)

Behan's absence is tolerable to the authorities in the first two
operations, but not in the third: death requires a body.

Schoolboy to master:

"Please, sir, can I be punished for something I haven't done?"

"Of course not."

"Thank you, sir. I'm afraid I haven't done my homework, sir."

The schoolboy is asking if he can be punished "for [doing]
something I haven't done," but perhaps it should have been put
"for not doing something that I should have done."

A silly person with a broken leg: "I tripped over a hole that was sticking up out of the ground."

By definition holes do not stick up, they go down. You break your leg on the rim, on the relation between the hole and the ground, the absence and presence of material.

A beggar of his tattered coat: "It's nothing but a parcel of holes sewn together."

We know that nothing is not what it appears to be. Undershirts made of a cellular fabric are warm because air is a poor conductor of heat.

"You know," said my grandmother Watson, "you could really feel the heat of that coat the minute you took it off."

She could feel it in comparison with her feelings when it was off—she felt it in the negative. She meant that one could feel the lost heat by taking it off. After all, cold is hot to the frozen stiff.

Two monks were drinking tea together, each boasting of the austerities to which he subjected himself.

"For instance," said one of them, "I drink tea without two lumps of sugar now."

An empty envelope that is sealed contains a secret.
Stanislaw Lec

"That's nothing," said the other. "I drink my tea without *six* lumps of sugar."

Without sugar is without sugar; it is unquantifiable. On the other hand, to have given up so much is to have given up more.

Just the omission of Jane Austen's books alone would make a fairly good library out of a library that hadn't a book in it. (Mark Twain)

To omit from the empty is Twain's strong rhetoric to deplore Austen.

20. Visual
NOTHING

To represent nothing one has to give it a certain shape. Méret Oppenheim's *Word, Wrapped in Poisonous Letters* (68) is a parcel of nothing given shape by the string that surrounds it. Nothing is there, but we imagine it to have a rectangular shape because the string is bent that way. One implication of this piece is that nothing is solid enough to force the string into that shape and keep it there. Nothing is solid enough to be mailed.

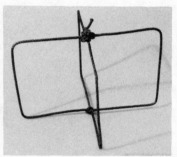

**68. Word, Wrapped in
Poisonous Letters**
(Méret Oppenheim)

A carnival novelty made of wired plastic that keeps the leash firm is the invisible dog (69), shown here being taken for a walk by the author. It takes its shape from the collar and the context. It is as if you can see the dog and nobody else can, a case of the emperor's new clothes. The illusion is greater in real life when the dog is actually walking. Then clues are given by the movement of the leash, the walker straining at the leash, and so on. Another joke is that there may have been a dog there, but as dogs go, it went.

69. The Invisible Dog
(photograph by Lawrence Lawry)

M. C. Escher's *Angels and Devils* (70) shows visually how evil is the negative of good. The devils' bat wings fit exactly in absolute opposition to the angels' bird wings and so on all through this picture.

70. Angels and Devils
(M. C. Escher)

Appendix:
GOLDWYNISMS

The film producer Samuel Goldwyn unconsciously made, consciously made, had made for him, or apocryphally made many bulls, known as Goldwynisms. Happily for the scheme of this book—for it provides some vindication of its system of categories—he made bulls that fit into all the categories here (except the mere pleonasm, which perhaps was not worth recording). He also made a number of malapropisms and mixed metaphors, which fall just outside the scope of this study.

Goldwyn was born in Poland in 1881, emigrated to Birmingham, England, at the age of twelve, came to the United States three years later in 1896, and died in 1974. There are several reasons why he made "mistakes" with the English language and idiom. He came fresh to the English language; he spoke Polish and Yiddish until he was twelve years old, and retained an accent all his life. He left school at eleven. He was often impatient, as movie producers are; it is easy to make approximations when you are in a hurry. He was egocentric and unselfconscious and somewhat inattentive to what others said. He was in a position to lay down the law to others. He was imaginative and often had a different, wider perspective on things. He perceived larger patterns and did not necessarily attend to the small details of language. To the extent that he consciously made bulls he certainly had a command of rhetoric; many of his remarks are powerfully put. It is said that some Goldwynisms were written for him and that he wanted to become well known for them. Arthur Marx says in his biography *Goldwyn: A Biography of the Man Behind the Myth*, from which many of these examples are taken:

It's a Hollywood legend that when Goldwyn first branched out on his own, he called in the head of his publicity department and said, "David Belasco became a famous producer by wearing a cape and his collar wrong-side around. What can I do to make myself famous?"

Marx quotes Irving Fein, who worked for a year as Goldwyn's assistant publicity director:

"Sure we used to make up Goldwynisms all the time in order to get publicity breaks. I remember one right now that I made up— 'Quick as a flashlight.'" (This is a malapropism on "quick as a flash.")

Marx also quotes George Oppenheimer, from the days when he was a Hollywood scriptwriter:

" 'It rolls off my back like a duck' was one of mine." (The proverb is "It rolls off me like water off a duck's back.")

When such quips are attributed to Goldwyn, there is an element of condescension toward the immigrant, just as there is in the attribution of bulls to the Irish and Polish.

Let us consider the Goldwynisms according to the scheme of this study.

Tautology

"We heard you're difficult," said Edgar Selwyn.

"Is that all?" asked Goldwyn.

"Some people even say you're disagreeable," added Selwyn.

"Listen," said Goldwyn, "just because I disagree with people doesn't mean I'm disagreeable."

"Disagree" and "disagreeable" are almost the same word, though they have now diverged in meaning, as Goldwyn points out.

Goldwyn, when told that his son was engaged to be married, replied: "Thank heaven. A bachelor's life is no life for a single man."

What Goldwyn meant was that a bachelor's life did not seem to him particularly to be desired: one should marry. He overemphasized; he might have said that a bachelor's life is not the life for a man.

Goldwyn was sitting up in bed and feeling strong enough to complain to his wife and the doctor:

"A hospital is no place to be sick. I'm dying of boredom in this place."

What Goldwyn meant was that it was not very pleasant to be sick in the hospital; it was boring and so on. In his vehemence he had forgotten "hospital" and its meaning by the time he got to "no place to be sick."

Samuel Goldwyn: "Our comedies are not to be laughed at!"

Goldwyn often used the English idiom unthinkingly. In this case "not to be laughed at" is a phrase used ironically to mean "of considerable merit." Goldwyn meant that his comedies should be regarded as serious efforts in the genre, and he did not notice the contradiction.

Oxymoron

Samuel Goldwyn (to a director): "I can give you a definite perhaps."

"Perhaps" means "possible but uncertain," while "definite" means "certain." Furthermore, a "perhaps" is not something you can give; it is not a noun. You can give a "definite no" or a "definite yes." Goldwyn bends the rules to give a "definite perhaps." Part of the humor of this line lies in our understanding of the movie business, the vacillations in the face of the large investments in fragile properties. Goldwyn meant to describe a genuine possibility.

Samuel Goldwyn (on being told a script was full of clichés): "Let's have some new clichés."

By definition a cliché is an old, tired expression; it cannot be new. It might have been that Goldwyn was told that the script was full of "tired old clichés" and took "cliché" simply to mean "idea" or "notion"; his relationship to the English language was that vague.

There are new clichés—ideas that very quickly become common-place and trendy.

Goldwyn asked D. W. Griffith to direct a picture for his company. "You say you've never made a picture before?" asked Griffith. "Yes," said Goldwyn, "but that is our strongest weak point."

His "strongest weak point" could indeed be a strength in that he had not made a picture before and might not be constrained by convention.

Contradiction in Terms

At a meeting of the Motion Picture Producers and Distributors of America that had been called to discuss the group's labor difficulties, Goldwyn disagreed with an important policy decision. He reached for his hat and exclaimed, "Gentlemen, include me out."

"Include me in" is the conventional tautology, which by its repetition gives an emphasis. The terms "include me" and "out" are contradictory.

Samuel Goldwyn: "A verbal contract isn't worth the paper it's written on."

A verbal contract is not written on paper. However, a verbal contract is often not worth very much. Goldwyn perhaps did not know what "verbal" meant; he may have thought that a verbal contract was simply an inferior contract.

Samuel Goldwyn: "I can tell you in two words: im possible."

Goldwyn is again seeking emphasis; he accentuates each syllable of "impossible," making it into two words. The term "in two words" does not accord with the one word "impossible."

"Mr. Goldwyn, my wife gave birth to a baby boy last night, and in honor of you, we're naming the baby Sam."

"Why do you want to do that?" snapped Goldwyn. "Every Tom, Dick, and Harry is named Sam."

Goldwyn again fails to attend to the small print in the saying "every Tom, Dick, and Harry," and he takes its meaning—"everyone ordinary"—rather than remaining aware of the precise words. Goldwyn was not at his best with names, words which form a special class in that they are specific to the objects named and not, as are other words, applicable in general. This is a contradiction in terms in that the terms "Tom, Dick, and Harry" do not accord with "Sam."

Samuel Goldwyn: "I paid too much for it, but it's worth it."

The terms "too much" and "worth it" are contradictory. But we know what Goldwyn means—a thing can be worth something economically or psychologically.

Samuel Goldwyn: "Gentlemen, for your information, I have a question to ask you."

One asks questions to gain information, not to give it. But there are questions like "Have you stopped beating your wife?" that give information. Information is at the other end of the spectrum of knowledge from questioning.

Samuel Goldwyn (of a script): "I read part of it all the way through."

To read a part of a thing is one thing; to read a thing all the way through is another. The way in which Goldwyn read the part was all the way through, intently, seriously. Goldwyn meant he could learn enough about the whole script from a close study of a detail.

Samuel Goldwyn: "If I could drop dead right now, I'd be the happiest man alive!"

Goldwyn is again being inattentive to the idiom, taking "If I could drop dead right now" in its meaning of "I am particularly pleased with events at the moment" and not seeing that it is contradictory with being the happiest man alive.

Samuel Goldwyn: "I never put on a pair of shoes until I've worn them at least five years."

Goldwyn is misled by his use of extravagant rhetoric. "Never" here is contrasted with "[wearing for] at least five years." He is trying both ways of persuading us that he has sensitive feet.

Samuel Goldwyn: "Let's bring it up-to-date with some snappy nineteenth-century dialogue."

Usually we say "snappy twentieth-century dialogue": "snappy" and "nineteenth-century" are held to be contradictory terms. Goldwyn is also reminding us of the way in which dialogue in the costume films of his time did sometimes seem to be anachronistically modern.

Mary Pickford: "You know something, Sam, your wife Frances has beautiful hands."

Samuel Goldwyn: "I know. Someday I'm going to have a bust made of them."

Goldwyn in his ignorance did not know that the term "bust" in sculpture does not simply mean a small sculpture, but a head and shoulders. He is saying "A head will be made of her hands."

Goldwyn: "What kind of dancing does Martha Graham do?"

Associate: "Modern dancing."

Goldwyn: "I don't want her then. Modern dancing is so old-fashioned."

Goldwyn takes the whole phrase "modern dancing" to mean what it meant at that time. It had become an overused cliché in his view.

Samuel Goldwyn: "I don't think anybody should write his autobiography until after he's dead."

Goldwyn did not know the difference between biography and autobiography. He may also have been confused between writing a book and publishing it.

The Obvious

Samuel Goldwyn: "The reason so many people showed up at Louis B. Mayer's funeral was because they wanted to make sure he was dead."

If Goldwyn made this gag, it shows his ability to make conscious bulls. The reason one goes to a funeral is that someone is dead. Goldwyn gives the remark the twist at "to make sure," as Mayer's death was apparently desired by some people. Another implication is that Mayer was so devious that he might even have deceived death.

The studio bookkeeper: "Mr. Goldwyn, our files are bulging with paperwork we no longer need. May I have your permission to destroy all our records before 1945?"

Goldwyn: "Certainly. Just be sure to keep a copy of everything."

There is a contradictory side to this story: all our records are to be destroyed, and a copy of everything is to be made and stored, are contradictory. The important element in the joke is the way in which the copies duplicate the records in an obvious way.

Samuel Goldwyn (stepping out one lovely morning onto the beach): "What a wonderful day to spend Sunday."

The Sun-day and the wonderful day come from the same root, day. It is almost the tautological "what a wonderful day to spend a day." Goldwyn is badly remembering a popular phrase with a hidden rhyme, "what a wonderful way to spend Sunday."

Samuel Goldwyn (after slicing five golf balls into the water hazard and finally making a long, straight drive to the green): "What did I do right?"

Usually the phrase is "What did I do wrong?" This is almost a figure/ground reversal; against a background of wrongs he asks what is right, rather than asking what is wrong against a background of rights.

Figure/Ground Reversal

Samuel Goldwyn (from the rail of a liner leaving New York for London, to his assembled relatives, friends, and employees): *"Bon voyage! Bon voyage!"*

Goldwyn knew *bon voyage* was the term used at parting on trips, but he did not know what it meant. He did not distinguish between the active voyager and the passive stay-at-homes. There is a resemblance to the railway train paradox in that he is presuming they are moving rather than he.

Self-Reference

Samuel Goldwyn: "Anyone who goes to a psychiatrist ought to have his head examined."

Since anyone who goes to a psychiatrist goes to have his head examined, this is a self-referential argument. The terms "going to a psychiatrist" and "having your head examined" are the same, except that one is pejorative.

Self-Contradiction

Samuel Goldwyn: "I had a monumental idea this morning, but I didn't like it."

This can be put: "I had a monumental idea this morning. I did not like the monumental idea I had this morning."

Thus Goldwyn contradicts himself. This bull contains his egotistical, changeable, contradictory nature. It is true to life—what seems a monumental idea can soon seem less than that.

Samuel Goldwyn (playing cards in his own house, and getting in a temper): "I've never been so insulted in my life—I'm going home."

You cannot go home if you are at home. In his excitement Goldwyn forgot where he was.

Mind and Matter

Samuel Goldwyn (on a film set of a tenement): "Why is everything so dirty here?"

The director: "Because it's supposed to be a slum area."

Goldwyn: "Well, this slum cost a lot of money. It should look better than an ordinary slum."

Goldwyn is arguing that a lifelike bit of art should look like life but more so. Goldwyn wants clean dirt.

Samuel Goldwyn: "Gentlemen, listen to me slowly!"

This antithesis between listening and speaking is a false one; usually we listen at the same speed as people speak. Listening does not have a speed; on the other hand, there are different speeds of perception. What we normally say is "Listen to me carefully." (Compare with the "trouble hearing/trouble listening" dichotomy on page 122.)

Nothing

A young author was granted a brief opportunity to tell Goldwyn a story he had written. Goldwyn fell asleep during the telling of the tale. The angry writer berated Goldwyn: "All I'm asking for is your opinion and you fall asleep!"

Samuel Goldwyn: "Isn't sleeping an opinion?"

The absence of attention is an opinion. (Compare with Rossini's remark to the young composer on page 181.) This story shows Goldwyn as quick-witted enough to explain his sleeping immediately on waking.

Mixed Metaphors

Goldwyn's ignorance of English idiom, coupled with his egocentric excitability, often led him into these mistakes.

Samuel Goldwyn: "That's the trouble with directors—always biting the hand that lays the golden egg."

He confuses "biting the hand that feeds them" with "killing the goose that lays the golden eggs." The hand that lays the egg is a fine image.

Samuel Goldwyn (to a director who had to make some difficult decisions): "You're the director. You should take the bull by the teeth."

This is a conflation of "take the bull by the horns" and "take the bit between the teeth." Both metaphors are obviously far from Goldwyn's experience. His new picture of taking the bull by the teeth is fresher, tighter, stronger.

Samuel Goldwyn (on Goldwynisms): "I can take them with a dose of salts."

This is a confusion of "I went through them like a dose of salts" and "I can take them with a pinch of salt." A dose of salts is a laxative, quickly purifying you; to take something with a pinch of salt is to doubt it, to take it lightly. To take them with a dose of salts is presumably to take them as lightly as a laxative.

Samuel Goldwyn: "Keep a stiff upper chin."

This is a mixture of "keep a stiff upper lip" and "take it on the chin." Chins are not upper, and they are usually quite stiff.

Samuel Goldwyn: "I resent anyone who attacks the ideology we live under—democracy. Believe me, I love the ground I walk on."

This is a version of "I worship the ground you walk on." Typically, it is self-centered.

Samuel Goldwyn: "He treats me like the dirt under my feet."

"He treats me like dirt" is combined with "to feel the earth under my feet."

Samuel Goldwyn: "We have all passed a lot of water since then."

Malapropisms

Samuel Goldwyn: ". . . we have that Indian scene. We can get the Indians right from the reservoir."

Mrs. Malaprop in Sheridan's *The Rivals* (1775) made errors of language through an attempt to seem learned; Goldwyn's mistakes are born of his self-confident ignorance. "Reservoir" for "reservation" is good: they are both artificial versions of the real.

Samuel Goldwyn (of Lillian Hellman's play *The Children's Hour*): "Maybe we ought to buy it?"

Merritt Hulburd: "Forget it, Mr. Goldwyn. It's about lesbians."

Samuel Goldwyn: "Don't worry about that. We'll make them Americans."

We do not know if Goldwyn was really as otherworldly as this. Goldwyn's idea is that lesbians are some national group—like Serbo-Croatians.

Jerry Chodorov: ". . . there's no telling how long the war will last."

Samuel Goldwyn: "Don't worry about that; the war's all over bar the shooting."

The hidden cliché here is "it's all over bar the shouting." Shooting is an integral part of modern warfare.

Samuel Goldwyn: "You don't realize what life is all about until

you have found yourself lying on the brink of a great abscess."

The brink of an abyss is probably more undesirable than a great abscess; an abscess sticks up, an abyss does the opposite.

Associate: "It's too caustic for films."

Samuel Goldwyn: "To hell with the cost. If it's a good story, I'll make it."

The punning confusion between "caustic" and "costly" shows Goldwyn's inability to distinguish between adjectival endings to nouns: we say "Pyrrhic" but not "costic."

Malapropisms of Proper Names

To Goldwyn, Ben Kahane, an executive at Columbia Pictures, was always "Mr. Cocoon"; Shirley Temple was Anne Shirley; King Vidor was Henry King; Joel McCrea was Jill McGraw; and Farley Granger was Ginger Farley.

Proper names, which have little meaning, often present a challenge to people who manipulate language. Goldwyn often could not be bothered to learn them.

Goldwyn saw "Valley of the Hello Dollies"; when he was filming *The Little Foxes* he called it "The Three Little Foxes," and he called *Wuthering Heights* "Withering Heights."

Brief Bibliography

Collections of Quotations

Auden, W. H., and Kronenberger, Louis. *The Faber Book of Aphorisms*, London: Faber & Faber, 1964; New York: Penguin Books, 1981.

Baldwin, Robert, and Paris, Ruth. *The Book of Similes*. London: Routledge and Kegan Paul, 1982.

Cohen, J. M., and Cohen, M. J. *The Penguin Dictionary of Quotations*. Harmondsworth: Penguin Books, 1971.

Green, Jonathon. *A Dictionary of Contemporary Quotations*. London: Pan Books, 1982.

Esar, Evan. *20,000 Quips and Quotes*. New York: Doubleday and Co., 1968.

Evans, Bergen. *Dictionary of Quotations*. New York: Avenel Books, 1978.

Fuller, Edmund. *2500 Anecdotes for All Occasions*. New York: Avenel Books, 1980.

———. *4800 Wisecracks for All Occasions*. New York: Avenel Books, 1980.

Henry, Lewis C. *Best Quotations for All Occasions*. New York: Fawcett Premier Books, 1965.

Hunt, Jonathon. *Dictionary of Quotations*. London: Hamlyn Publishing Group, 1979.

Hyman, Robin. *A Dictionary of Famous Quotations*. London: Bell and Hyman, 1978.

Ivens, Michael, and Dunstan, Reginald. *Bachman's Book of Freedom Quotations*. London: Bachman and Turner, 1978.

Mencken, H. L. *Dictionary of Quotations*. New York: Knopf, 1942.

Murphy, Edward F. *The Macmillan Treasury of Relevant Quotations*. London: Macmillan, 1979.

———. *2715 One-Line Quotations*. New York: Crown, 1981.

The Concise Oxford Dictionary of Quotations. Oxford: Oxford University Press, 1964.

Peter, Lawrence J. *Quotations for Our Time*. London: Souvenir Press, 1978.

Rosten, Leo. *Infinite Riches*. New York: McGraw-Hill, 1979.

———. *Treasury of Jewish Quotations*. New York: McGraw-Hill, 1972.

Spiegelman, Art, and Schneider, Bob. *Whole Grains—A Book of Quotations*. New York: Quick Fox, 1973.

Tripp, Rhoda Thomas. *The International Thesaurus of Quotations*. Harmondsworth: Penguin Books, 1976.

Collections of Jokes

Butler, Tony. *Best Irish Jokes*. London: Wolfe Publishing, 1968.

———. *More Best Irish Jokes*. London: Wolfe Publishing, 1970.

Cagney, Peter. *Positively the Last Irish Joke Book*. London: Futura Publications, 1979.

Chambers, Garry. *The Complete Irish Gag Book*. London: W. H. Allen, 1979.

Dickson, Paul. *The Official Rules*. London: Arrow Books, 1980.

Edwards, Kenneth. *More things I wish I'd said, and some I wish I hadn't*. London: Abelard-Schuman, 1978.

Fantoni, Barry. *Colemanballs*. London: André Deutsch, 1982.

Hornby, Peter. *The Official Irish Joke Book*. London: Futura Publications, 1977.

———. *The Official Irish Joke Book No. 3*. London: Futura Publications, 1979.

Rees, Nigel. *Graffiti Lives, OK*. London: Unwin Paperbacks, 1979.

Collections of Bulls

Benayoun, Robert. *Le Taureau Irlandais*. Paris: Filipacchi, 1974.

Edgeworth, Maria, and Edgeworth, Richard Lovell. *Essay on Irish Bulls*. London, 1808.

Jerrold, Walter. *Bulls, Blunders and Howlers*. London, 1929.

Neilson, G. R. *The Book of Bulls*. London, 1898.

Percy, James C. *Bulls Ancient and Modern*. London, 1912.
———. *Bulls and Blunders*. London, 1915.
———. *More Bulls and Blunders*. London, 1921.

On Rhetoric

Bombaugh, C. C. *Oddities and Curiosities of Words and Literature*. New York: Dover, 1961.
Bullinger, E. W. *Figures of Speech Used in the Bible*. Grand Rapids, Mich.: Baker Book House, 1968.
Lanham, Richard A. *A Handlist of Rhetorical Terms*. Berkeley and Los Angeles: University of California Press, 1969.
Paulos, John Allen. *Mathematics and Humor*. Chicago: University of Chicago Press, 1980.

Collection of Goldwynisms

Marx, Arthur. *Goldwyn: A Biography of the Man Behind the Myth*. New York: W. W. Norton & Co., 1976.

On Oxymoron

Freytag, Wiebke. *Das Oxymoron bei Wolfram, Gottfried und andern Dichtern des Mittelalters*. Munchen: Wilhelm Fink Verlag, 1972.

Collections of Drawings

Baxter, Glen. *The Impending Gleam*. London: Jonathan Cape, 1981.
Sternberg, Jacques, and Caen, Michael, eds. *Les Chefs-d'oeuvre du dessin d'humour*. Paris: Éditions Planète, 1968.

Collections of Aphorisms and Visual Aphorisms

Earnshaw, Anthony. *Flick Knives and Forks*. Sidmouth, Devon: Transformaction, 1982.

Mariën, Marcel. *Crystal Blinkers*. Sidmouth, Devon: Transformaction, 1976.

By the Same Author

Hughes, Patrick, and Brecht, George. *Vicious Circles and Infinity: An Anthology of Paradoxes*. New York: Penguin Books, 1979.

——— and Hammond, Paul. *Upon the Pun: Dual Meaning in Words and Pictures*. London: W. H. Allen, 1978.

Grateful acknowledgment is made for permission to reproduce and reprint the following:

Drawing by Chas. Addams reproduced by permission of *The New Yorker*. Copyright © The New Yorker Magazine, Inc., 1975.

"The Queen Mary" reproduced by permission of Barnaby's Picture Library.

Man Sawing by Glen Baxter reproduced by permission of Glen Baxter.

Corset-Bastille by Hans Bellmer reproduced by permission of the Association pour la Diffusion des Arts Graphiques et Plastiques.

Buster Keaton's Anchor and *Brokedown Lorry* by Tony Blundell reproduced by permission of Tony Blundell.

Lolly/tongue and *Cut Along the Dotted Line* by Les Coleman reproduced by permission of Les Coleman.

The Persistence of Memory by Salvador Dali reproduced by permission of The Museum of Modern Art.

Why Not Sneeze, Rose Selavy? by Marcel Duchamp reproduced by permission of the Philadelphia Museum of Art: The Louise and Walter Arensberg Collection.

Raider's Bread, Snowman on a Bonfire, and *Unicorn with a Carrot* by Anthony Earnshaw reproduced by permission of Anthony Earnshaw.

Angels and Devils by M. C. Escher reproduced by permission of Visual Artists and Galleries Association, Inc. Copyright © BEELDRECHT, Amsterdam/V.A.G.A., New York, Collection Haags Gemeentemusem—The Hague, 1981.

Persecution and Mass Murder (*Politiska Röster* [*Political Voices*]) by Falk/Bergentz/Lenskog reproduced by permission of Swedish Radio and the Cultural Department, Swedish Embassy.

Marble Paper Boat by Ian Hamilton Finlay reproduced by permission of Ian Hamilton Finlay.

Drawing by Jean Gourmelin reproduced by permission of Jean Gourmelin.

Drawing by "H" reproduced by permission of *The New Yorker*. Copyright © The New Yorker Magazine, Inc., 1952, 1980.

Drawings by Maurice Henry reproduced by permission of Maurice Henry.

Apple Tree by Bianca Juarez reproduced by permission of Bianca Juarez.

Sealskin Seal, Waves in the Sand, Concrete Bag, Ceramic Flowers, Stone Angel, Stone Book, Floating Sugar, Rubber Pencil, Magic Wand, Limp Magic Wand, Spilled Ink, Photograph of Waves, and *The Invisible Dog* by Lawrence Lawry reproduced by